AF530569

An Introduction to Stylistics

Theory and Practice

Partha Sarathi Misra

Orient BlackSwan

An Intorduction to Stylistics : Theory and Practice

ORIENT BLACKSWAN PRIVATE LIMITED

Registered Office
3-6-752, Himayatnagar, Hyderabad 500 029 Telangana, India
E-mail: centraloffice@orientblackswan.com

Other Offices
Bangalore, Bhopal, Chennai, Ernakulam, Guwahati, Hyderabad, Jaipur, Kolkata, Lucknow, Mumbai, New Delhi, Noida, Patna, Vijayawada

First Published 2009
Reprinted 2009, 2012, 2015, 2016

ISBN: 978- 81-250-3678-4

Typeset in 10.5/13 pt Sabon

Typeset by
System Graphics (India) Private Limited, New Delhi

Printed at
Bluebells Secure Prints
Hyderabad 500 018

Published by
Orient Blackswan Private Limited
3-6-752, Himayatnagar, Hyderabad 500 029 Telangana, India
E-mail: hyderabad@orientblackswan.com.

Contents

Introduction

An Introduction to Stylistics is an introductory reader in stylistics meant for initiating readers in general and students in particular to the basic theories and practices of stylistics. The book aims at equipping readers with the tools required for a stylistic interpretation of literary as well as non-literary discourses. The book also tries to narrow the gap between the study of language and literature and propagates an integrated study of both.

Though there is a growing worldwide interest in the relevance of a stylistic approach to the study of literature, readers are often baffled by the contradictory theories propounded by the votaries of stylistics. While some books stress upon the methodological approach of stylistics in the study of literature, its rigidity and objectivity is often decried. This book avoids contentious issues raised by the critics of stylistics, as its primary objective is to help readers form a strong foundation in the subject.

A distinguishing feature of the book is its emphasis on the use of stylistic tools in the interpretation of literary as well as non-literary texts. The detailed analysis of a number of poems, short stories and drama texts will serve as models for any stylistic analysis of literary texts. A chapter on the stylistic analysis of the language of English newspapers published in India has also been included to demonstrate the efficacy of stylistics in the domain of non-literary texts. The present book we hope will prompt readers to explore the wonderful world of literary as well as non-literary texts with the help of stylistics.

1

Stylistics and the Interpretation of Literature

1.1 STYLISTICS, LINGUISTICS AND LITERARY CRITICISM

Stylistics, a major branch of linguistics, is primarily concerned with the application of the methodology of linguistics to the study of the style used in language in a particular context. We use language, whether in speech or writing for a particular purpose and choose our words accordingly. While transmitting a message, we select language from an array of syntactical and lexical possibilities to relate the style with the purpose of communication.

Stylistics is not concerned solely with written language. It is also equally important in the domain of spoken discourse. But literary critics and votaries of stylistics are generally interested in the study of stylistics with reference to the written discourse. In *Stylistics and the Teaching of Literature* (1975) H.G. Widdowson defines stylistics as the 'study of literary discourse from a linguistic orientation'. He denies stylistics an autonomous domain of its own, and states that stylistics is an intermediary between literary criticism and linguistics. He points out that etymologically the 'style' component of the word 'stylistics' comes from literary criticism and the 'istics' component comes from linguistics. He goes on to say that 'stylistics can provide a way of mediating between two subjects, English language and literature.'

While the literary critic is interested in the interpretation of the codes used in a discourse, the linguist is interested in studying the actual codes used in the message of the discourse. Stylistics is a bridge between the literary critic and the linguist and makes a synthesis of the literary critic's observations and the linguist's literary intuitions. While a linguist treats a discourse as an example of the language system, the literary critic tries to find out the underlying significance of a discourse.

The linguist's primary concern is the text as a linguistic entity, a piece of language with communicative dynamics that are encoded in the text. From the linguists' point of view, the language of an advertisement is as complex as that of a poem, and they are not interested in finding out if it is a valuable representation of human experience. Consider these two texts:

> Yes. You are in good company when you bank with us. Because you may not be our biggest customer but at ITB we will make you feel like one.
> You will benefit from our innovative products which meet all your needs. Our technology ensures that you enjoy the convenience and time-saving banking that we offer.
>
> If you are not banking with us, call us today and experience a new way of banking.

> O Rose, thou art sick!
> The invisible worm,
> That flies in the night,
> In the howling storm,
>
> Has found out thy bed
> Of crimson joy;
> And his dark secret love
> Does thy life destroy.

Both the texts serve some communicative purposes. A literary critic is interested in the second text as it represents a human experience. Evaluating the text, he will determine why and how it succeeds or fails as a work of art. A linguist will be interested in both the texts; he will not discriminate between the literary and the non-literary texts. Scholars interested in stylistics will also be interested in both the texts, but unlike the literary critics they will not account for the literary value of the texts.

The second text is quoted from Blake's *Songs of Experience*. If we change the graphology of the text it will read as 'O Rose, thou art sick! The invisible worm, that flies in the night, in the howling storm, has found out thy bed of crimson joy and his secret love does thy love destroy'. Does the change of the graphology affect the communicative value of the second text? Which graphological presentation serves a better communicative purpose, the first or the second?

Style is a distinctive way of using language to convey the intended meaning in an appropriate manner and stylistics is the study of the distinctive expressions of language from a linguistic orientation.

When we investigate the style of a text we try to find out three main stylistic levels: the linguistic form or the substance of the text, the discourse of the text and the communicative situation of the text. These three levels can be presented as follows:

1. Macro-level—communicative situation
2. Intermediate level—the discourse of the text
3. Micro-level —the linguistic form

In order to unfold the mystery of a text we begin our investigation at the micro-level and proceed towards the macro-level.

Language serves different communicative roles or functions in literary as well as in non-literary texts. While going by road to a hill station in India, motorists often come across notices like the following:

> Better to be Mr Late than the Late Mr.
> If you are married, divorce speed.
> Speed thrills but kills.

These notices aim at ensuring the safety of the motorists who are often tempted to drive rashly. While the first and the third notices seem to be general statements they are actually directives to motorists. The second notice is a direct appeal to motorists. Thus, though there is a variation in style all the notices serve the same communicative purpose; they warn the rash motorist of the perils of reckless driving on mountain roads. Now, consider the following statement, is it meant for thanking the people or is it a warning?

Thank you for not smoking.

If we see this sentence written at the entrance of a room we realise that smoking is not allowed. The word 'thank' may not always thank, it can instruct or warn as well.

While discussing different functions of language of a text Halliday (1967) mentions three distinct functions or communicative roles of language. They are: *textual, ideational* and *interpersonal*. The study of the textual function aims at finding out how the linguistic units cohere together to make a text. The study of the ideational function involves an enquiry into the representation of reality in a text. At the interpersonal level we try to find out how the text tries to establish a relationship with the readers. This relationship or the *tenor* between the person initiating the text (the addresser) and the addressee or the person for whom the text is intended is a crucial factor at the macro-level of study. A text, whether literary or non-literary, is a message sent by a sender to a receiver. It is embedded in a context and exists in a setting. It follows a particular code, verbal or non-verbal, and is transmitted in a mode, written or spoken.

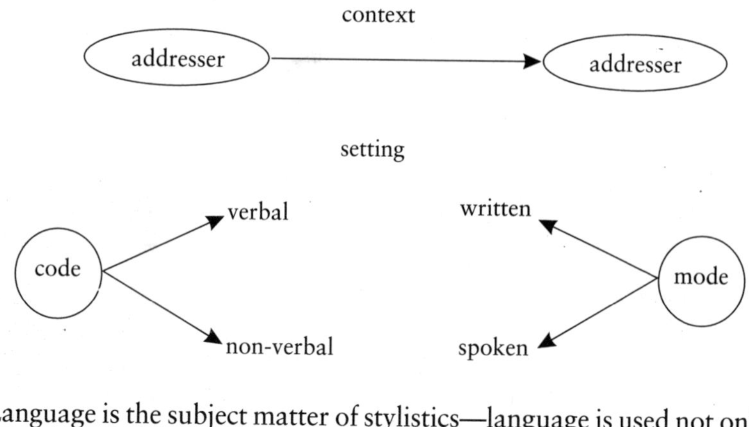

Language is the subject matter of stylistics—language is used not only in literary composition, but in everyday conversation, in scientific reports and all sorts of communication. The world of the literary critic is confined to a small branch of linguistic communication, which is thought worthy of preservation as literature. Both literary criticism and stylistics describe and explain linguistic communication, but their goals are different.

1.2 STYLISTICS AND STYLE

Lexically speaking, stylistics is the systematic study of style used in language. This abstruse definition prompts us to look for the lexical meaning of style. Style, according to the lexicon, is the way of doing something, especially one that is typical of a person, a group of people, a place or a period. The notion of style, therefore, implies the existence of two mediums. Style cannot exist in a vacuum, and as stylistics is the systematic study of style used in language we can presume that stylistics also cannot exist as a discipline all by itself.

Stylistics has received a lot of attention in recent years from literary critics, linguists and the teachers of language and literature. While some have eulogised it as an effective tool for exploring the web of words presented in literary as well as non-literary discourses; others have viewed it as an unreliable key to unfold the mystery of numerous discourse types produced by the readers or the writers of a particular language.

Style in language arises due to the possibility of choice among alternative forms of expression. We may refer to a person as a *man*, a *guy* or a *bloke*, and the choice among these three forms of expression will be conditioned by the stylistic effect that we intend to make in a particular context.

The question of choice is related to the personality and the mental state of the speaker or the writer, and, therefore, the style is often seen as a distinguishing mark of character. Our personality plays an important role in the making of choice in our use of language. Jane asks Lucy, "Did you notice the new commercial building on G.S Road?" Lucy replies, "No, it was never noticed by me." Lucy could say, 'Sorry, I didn't.', but she preferred a passive sentence to create a distancing effect. We also use a sentence in the passive voice if we intend to be non-committal. A typical 'character certificate' issued by a person having a responsible position in India often ends with the following sentence:

Nothing is known against his character.

What is the difference between the following sentences?

I don't know anything against his character

Nothing is known against his character.

It is stylistics alone that can give us a clue to the writer's personality and the choices that he makes.

Stylistics applies linguistics to literary as well as non-literary texts and attempts to formulate principles capable of explaining the particular choices made by writers, individuals and social groups in their use of language. While expressing oneself in a particular language, the speaker or the writer has a number of choices available to him, and depending on the situation he chooses a particular way of expression. The creativity of language presents a variety of options to the users and it is up to the users to select a particular variety that suits their purpose best. Let us take the following utterances made by a speaker:

Help.
Help, please.
Will you help me, please?
Would you help me, please?
Can you help me, please?
Could you help me, please?
I wonder if you could help me, please.

A speaker may utter any of these utterances asking for help, but his choice of a particular utterance will be conditioned by the context in which he makes the utterance. If his house is on fire, he will not use the last utterance to seek the assistance of his neighbours. The intuitive knowledge of the appropriate code of the language will guide him in his choice of the appropriate utterance.

As already stated, the interface between language and literature is the primary concern of stylistics. Roman Jakobson((1960) considers style as an inherent property of literary texts and calls for an explicit objective and structuralist stylistics. He, however, excludes the reader from the ambit of his notion of stylistics. The kind of stylistics advocated by Jakobson and his followers is known as 'formalist stylistics' as their sole objective was to study the intricate patterning of literary texts. Jakobson and his followers studied the patterning of literary texts, tried to find out the instances of repetition, parallelism and deviation noticed in a literary text, but while doing so, they failed to account for the correlation between the objective description of a literary text and its interpretation. The gap between analysis and interpretation remained elusive for the votaries of formalist stylistics.

The limitations of 'formalist stylistics' gave birth to 'functional stylistics'. This new approach tried to narrow the gap between analysis and interpretation by making the stylistic analysis of a text functional. The proponents of 'functional stylistics' considered a formal stylistic feature relevant only when it was functional from the point of view of interpretation. The functionalists recognised as stylistically significant those linguistic features of a text, which had stylistic effects or values.

Stylistics is not merely a linguistic analysis of a text. Stylistics uses linguistic tools to identify the linguistic features of the discourse that produce a certain aesthetic response in the writer or the reader. Let us go through the following extracts collected from different sources and try to find out the features that make them distinct:

1. Hi, I have got some great news. You know I watch the UGC programme on television every morning. Well, last Saturday the most amazing thing happened. My sister and I were watching the programme when the telephone rang. I felt annoyed, but answered it grudgingly. Well, you will never guess who it was! It was the great... , the legendary figure of the big screen. I couldn't believe it!
2. Two Japanese officers and a Filipino crewman kidnapped during a pirate attack in the Malacca Strait have been released unhurt in southern Thailand after being held captive for almost a week, officials said on Monday. The three men, looking exhausted and close to tears, later told a news conference how they were switched among fishing boats, marched through a jungle and then dumped into a boat at sea.
3. She danced next with an officer, and had the refreshment of talking of Wickham, and of hearing that he was universally liked. When

those dances were over she returned to Charlotte Lucas, and was in conversation with her, when she found herself suddenly addressed by Mr Darcy, who took her so much by surprise in his application for her hand, that, without knowing what she did, she accepted him. He walked away again immediately, and she was left to fret over her own want of presence of mind; Charlotte tried to console her.

4. For two nights and three days you will be pampered and cared for beyond imagination. Experience some of the most exotic locations, discover the magic of romance and rejuvenate body and mind with our spa treatments. Long after you have returned to real life, the unforgettable experience of staying at a Paradise Resort will remain a vivid memory.
5. Fasten your seat belts tightly around you once you are seated. Learn how to release the seat belts without fumbling. The release buckle is in front and it has to be lifted more than 90 degrees to unfasten it. Keep your seat upright and tray table stowed, when instructed to do so by the cabin staff to avoid injury if the aircraft comes to a sudden and unexpected halt.
6. Subjects to the limits of liability as laid in the Schedule hereto the Company will indemnify the insured in the event of an accident caused by or arising out of the use of the vehicle against all sums, which the insured shall become legally liable to pay.

After going through the six texts cited above, a reader familiar with the varieties of English will point out that the first extract is written in a colloquial informal style while the second extract is from a newspaper. Similarly, a reader is likely to comment that while the third extract may be a piece of literature the fourth one is an advertisement. A discerning reader will note that the fifth extract is from an instructional material published by an airline, and the sixth extract is a specimen of legal English. All these texts are unique and distinctive. Looking at all these texts we are sure to ask ourselves a question, 'What is it that makes one variety distinctive, and different from the other?' To answer this question we have to depend on the theory and practice of stylistics. Our primary response to any text written in a language is always intuitive. When we encounter a text beginning with a sentence like, 'Our source of inspiration who left us today...' we immediately know that it is taken from an obituary column. Though we can respond to a text intuitively we cannot account for our intuitive responses without a proper training in stylistics.

Language does not exist in a vacuum. It is used in a time, a place and in a cultural and cognitive context. As stylistics is the study of language in use it has to take into account the spatio-temporal, cultural and cognitive context in which a text (both literary and non-literary) occurs. Read the following texts and try to find out the context in which they occur.

House votes in favour of fuel hike
Rice rocks, rustles up knotty affair
ULFA attacks ASP, 7 hurt

Unhurried
    Unparalleled
Unstandardised
    Unspoilt
Unstressed
    Untainted
Untouched
    Untried
Untroubled
    Unexpected
Unrivalled
    Unconfined
    Until I came here
I thought words beginning with 'un'
    referred to things negative

The first is a newspaper headline of *Jakarta Post*, published from Jakarta, the second is from the Guwahati edition of the *Times of India*, the third is from the *Sentinel* published from Guwahati, and the fourth is an advertisement of the Maharastra Tourism Development Corporation.

On the basis of our discussion so far we can identify three key aspects of stylistics. They are:

1. Stylistics uses linguistics to approach a literary text.
2. Stylistics analyses texts on the basis of objective outlines rather than according to purely subjective and impressionistic values.
3. Stylistics puts emphasis on the aesthetic properties of language.

Stylistics studies the relation between language and its artistic function and in order to achieve this goal it depends on a set of linguistic tools. By applying the methodology of linguistics to the study of style used in language, stylistics helps us in decoding a message on a scientific basis. While acknowledging the role played by linguistics on stylistics we have to remember that stylistics is not just ticking off of some linguistic features of a text; linguistic forms of a text are taken into account only when they perform a communicative function.

1.3 STYLISTICS: AN INTERDISCIPLINARY FIELD

The publication of T.A. Sebeok's *Style in Language* in 1960 is usually considered to be a starting point for the growth of stylistics in England and America. The developments in linguistics in the sixties and the seventies gave a new impetus to stylistics and controversies about the relevance of linguistics to stylistics and literary criticism reached its climax during this period. There is, of course, no point in being dogmatic about the relevance of linguistics to stylistics. Linguistics has been a launching pad for stylistics and the latter is never conditioned or controlled by linguistic jargon. A text can be interpreted from different perspectives and, therefore, any dependence on a particular theoretical framework is likely to condition our interpretative skills. Stylistics has emerged as an interdisciplinary field of study in recent years and this is due to the eclectic approach advocated by its votaries.

Carter (1982) and Toolan (1988) also believe that stylistics can build bridges between the traditionally divided disciplines of language studies and literary studies. Literature provides a context for language use and stylistics points out the ways in which language study can reinforce the analysis of literary texts just as literature can help language study.

1.4 SUMMING UP

Stylistics, the study of style in written or spoken language has established itself as a distinct discipline with the help of its objective, the methodological approach to the study of language. The use of language in any communication, written or spoken, is highly structured and stylistics tries to unfold the structure of a message systematically without being influenced by subjective considerations. Stylistics explores the creativity in language use and therefore, the use of stylistics in the study of a discourse enhances the readers' sensitivity to language which leads to a fuller understanding of the meaning of the text. Stylistics is basically a method of textual interpretation based on a systematic analysis of the different linguistic features of the text. As style is a distinctive way of using language to convey the intended meaning in an appropriate manner, stylisticians aim at exploring the web of language to unearth the meaning of the text on a solid foundation.

Exercises

1. Define stylistics. How is it related to linguistics and literary criticism?
2. What, according to Halliday, are the three communicative roles of language?
3. What do you mean by 'functional stylistics'?
4. Do you think that stylistics can bridge the gap between 'language studies' and 'literary studies'?
5. Why is linguistics called a 'launching pad for stylistics'?

2

The Basic Assumptions of Stylistics

2.1 DEFINING STYLISTICS

Stylistics is a process of a literary text analysis which starts from a basic assumption that the primary interpretative procedures used in the reading of a literary text are linguistic procedures. While reading a text we react to it intuitively, and this initial response is basically a response to the language of the text. Stylistics helps us in formalising this initial response to a text, systematically. In order to validate our intuitive responses to a text, we need an analytic knowledge of the rules and conventions of normal linguistic communication. When a systematic analysis of the language of a text is undertaken to account for the intuitive responses to the text, it is bound to be less impressionistic and subjective. Stylistic analysis provides the means whereby we can relate a piece of literary writing to our own experience of language.

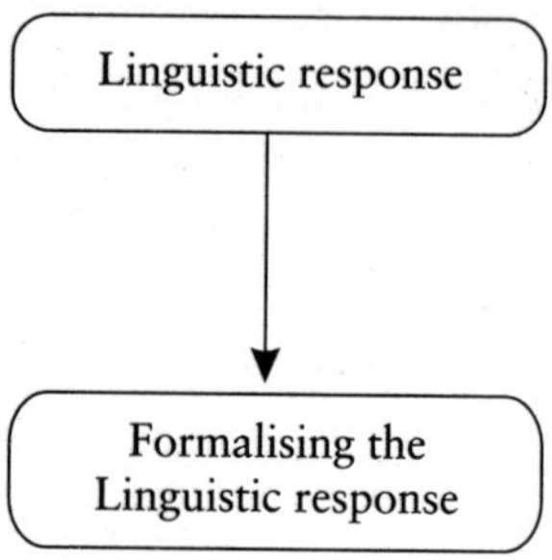

In his book *Language and Literature: An Introductory Reader in Stylistics*(1982) Ronald Carter remarks that stylistic analysis can provide the means whereby students of literature can relate a piece of literary writing to their own experience of language and so can extend that experience. It can assist in the transfer of interpretative skills, which is one of the essential purposes of literary education; stylistics provides systematic procedures for demystifying a literary or a non-literary discourse. These procedures are replicable, and they act as a guide in deciphering the message of a discourse. A reader's capacity to respond to language, however, is not dependent on language alone; it may be conditioned by personal, cultural or geographical experience of the particular reader.

Intuitive responses to a discourse are central to the process of stylistic analysis. They are a starting point for a fuller investigation of what a discourse means to a listener or a reader. It is assumed that constant exposure to the language in which a message is communicated is essential for a proper intuitive response to the language. In order to formalise our intuitions systematically, we should first learn how to analyse a language. A linguistic analysis of a text is a means of formulating intuitions. A firm basis in language analysis prompts a reader to proceed with precision in the analysis of a text, and makes him sensitive to the *what* and *how* of a text. Carter points out that without an analytic knowledge of the rules and conventions of normal linguistic communication, it is not possible for the readers to respond intuitively to a text. A systematic and explicit knowledge of the communicative and linguistic norms of the language in which a message is conveyed is a prerequisite for a stylistic analysis of a text.

What do we mean by an intuitive response to a text and how do we formalise the response? The following points of the principles and practice of stylistics formulated by Ronald Carter are crucial for students of stylistics:

1. that the greater our detailed knowledge of the working of the language system, the greater our capacity for insightful awareness of the effects produced by literary texts;

2. that a principled analysis of language can be used to make our commentary on the effects produced in a literary work less impressionistic and subjective;
3. that because it will be rooted in a systematic awareness of language, bits of language will not be merely spotted and evidence gathered in an essentially casual and haphazard manner. Statements will be made with recognition of the fact that analysis of one linguistic pattern requires reference to, or checking against, related patterns across the text.

Our earlier observation regarding the intuitive response to a text and the formalising of the responses can now be modified on the basis of these three principles and practices of stylistics mentioned above.

1. intutive response
2. analysing the language
3. adducing linguistic facts to substantiate intutions
4. making stylistic judgements

2.2 The Tools of Stylistics

Analysing a language is not an easy task. The patterns of the language, its grammatical structures, the large vocabulary, different types of discourses and numerous contexts in which these discourses take place are too daunting even for an expert in stylistics. Again, different analysts can describe the language of a text in different ways. The social, historical and cultural background of a discourse again may condition the intuitive responses of a reader. Therefore, in order to make stylistics easily accessible to readers, the following tools of stylistics are discussed in this chapter:

1. Sounds (alliteration, combination of sounds)
2. Lexis (words, word structures and interrelations)
3. Semantics (meaning relationships)
4. Discourse (structure of linguistic interaction)
5. Context (situational constraints)
6. Syntax (sentence structure)

2.2.1. Sounds

The sounds of a language used stylistically may create a particular literary and aesthetic effect on the reader or the listener. While we come across a particular discourse we are indirectly influenced by the sounds and the sound patterns used by the speaker or the writer. The sounds of a language may be studied with special reference to the speaker, the context, the surrounding air or the listener.

Segmental as well as supra-segmental features of a language affect the stylistic effect of a discourse. A professor in Guwahati narrated the following incident: The professor's neighbour had a domestic help named Deepali. She was so indispensable in the household that his neighbour'wife used to call for her a hundred times a day and the his ear was attuned to the sound effect of the word 'Deepali'. One morning the professor woke up on hearing the loud cry of his neighbour's wife. She was saying *Deepalik loi gol.* (Some one has kidnapped Deepali.) The professor ran out to find out what had happened and to his utter surprise learnt that his neighbour's wife was just looking for Deepali *Deepali koloi gol*? (Where is Deepali?/ Where has Deepali gone?) The absent-minded professor had missed the *pause* after the word Deepali, and consequently the interrogative sentence *Deepali koloi gol?* was decoded by him as an exclamatory sentence *Deepalik loi gol!*

That pause changes the meaning in a spoken discourse is evident in the following two sentences:

> My uncle who lives in Thailand has come.
> My uncle (pause) who lives in Thailand (pause) has come.

If we utter the first sentence without having a pause after 'My uncle' it will mean that I have one and only one uncle in Thailand. But if we pause after 'My uncle' and say 'My uncle... who lives in Thailand... has come' it will imply that I have more than one uncle and that the particular uncle who lives in Thailand has come.

We often talk of music in poetry. How does a poem acquire this musical quality? It is the sound effect of a discourse that makes it musical. Let us consider the musical qualities of the following poem:

In Xanadu did Kubla Khan
A stately pleasure-dome decree:
Where Alph, the sacred river, ran
Through caverns measureless to man
Down to a sunless sea.

The patterning of the sounds heightens the musical qualities of the lines mentioned above. The last words of all the four lines alliterate to one of the words closely preceding them.

Kubla	Khan
dome	decree
river	ran
measureless	man
sunless	sea

Besides alliteration, there is an intermittent occurrence of the /n/ sound in the last two lines: *ran, caverns, man, down, sunless*.

Consider the rapid rhythmic movement of a train described by Robert Louis Stevenson in the following lines of the poem *From a Railway Carriage*:

Faster than fairies, faster than witches
Bridges and houses, hedges and ditches;
And charging along like troops in a battle,
All through the meadows the horses and cattle:
All of the sights of the hill and the plain
Fly as thick as driving rain;
And ever again, in the wink of an eye,
Painted stations whistle by.

The echo of the sounds made by a moving train has been very aptly captured in the sound pattern of the poem. The quick movement suggested in the line *Faster than fairies, faster than witches* alternates with the slow movement of the second line *Bridges and houses, hedges and ditches*. Again, the quick movement of the third line *And charging along like troops in a battle* alternates with the slow movement of the line *All through the meadows the horses and cattle*. The symmetry of the first four lines is broken in the next four lines. The fifth line is slow in movement while the sixth line suggests a very quick movement.

Similarly, the seventh line is rather slow in movement, but it is compensated by the eighth line, *Painted stations whistle by.* The sound pattern may be expressed in the following manner:

1. Quick	2. Slow
3. Quick	4. Slow
5. Slow	6. Quick
7. Slow	8. Quick

2.2.2 Lexis

Lexis is a general term for vocabulary. Ronald Carter (1982) states that the study of the lexis of a text may be the starting point of a stylistic analysis of a text. Lexical items are associated in a text through shared semantic features. Let us take the following poem as an example and see how the study of the lexis gives us valuable clues to the meaning of the poem:

> Beside yon straggling fence that skirts the way,
> With blossom'd furze unprofitably gay
> There, in his noisy mansion, skil'd to rule
> The village master taught his little school.
> A man severe he was, and stern to view,
> I knew him well, and every truant knew;
> Well had the boding tremblers learned to trace,
> The day's disasters in his morning face;
> Full well they laughed with counterfeited glee,
> At all his jokes, for many a joke had he.
> Full well the busy whisper circling round
> Conveyed the dismal tiding when he frowned;
> Yet he was kind, or if severe in aught,
> The love he bore to learning was in fault;
> The village all declared how much he knew;
> 'Twas certain he could write and cipher too:
> Lands he could measure, terms and tides presage,
> And e'en the story ran that he could gauge,
> In arguing too, the parson owned his skill,
> For, e'en though vanquished, he could argue still,
> While words of learned length, and thundering sound

> Amazed the gazing rustics ranged around
> And still they gazed, and still the wonder grew
> That one small head could carry all he knew.

A study of the lexical items indicates two lexical chains: one for two types of images: visual and auditory; and the other for presenting the school and the pupils.

Visual	Auditory
straggling fence	noisy mansion
blossom'd furze	laughed
morning face	all his jokes
when he frowned	whisper
gazing rustics	argue still
one small head	thunderous sound
the school	the pupils
noisy mansion	truant
little school	boding trembles

A lexical chain is a sequence of related words in the text and is independent of the grammatical structure of the text. A lexical chain creates the context in which a message is transmitted by the addresser to the addressee. Any communication has a central theme or focus, and the lexical chain acts as a unifying force. The notion of lexical chaining is derived from the work of Halliday and Hasan (1976) in the field of textual cohesion, which will be discussed in the next section. A lexical chain may be created in a text by the repetition of the lexical items or by the use of synonyms, near-synonyms or semantically related words. Consider the lexical chain in the following text:

> Once upon a time there was a little **boy** and a little **girl**. **They** had a cat. Their **father** was an old man who loved pets. The little **kitten** was very cute and the **children** liked her very much. They fed her with care and played with her. The **kitten** also liked the little **boy** and the little girl. She used to mew when the **brother** and the **sister** stroked her gently. The **father** also took utmost care to make the little cat

comfortable. They were a happy family the father, his two children and the little kitten.

boy	pets	little boy
girl	cat	little girl
children	kitten	little kitten
brother	pussy	
sister	mew	
father		
family		

2.2.3 Semantics

According to Ferdinand de Saussure (1916), a word combines two elements: a sound image that is the physical form, and a sense or meaning. He refers to the sound image as the 'signifier' and the sense as the 'signified'. For Saussure, words are nothing but signs, and their relationship to the outside world is symbolic. The signifier is a label for a concept; it is not a label for an object. Saussure points out that there is no direct relationship between the sound of a word and the object it refers to. The signifier and the signified jointly refer to the outside world. Therefore, it is implied that words have two kinds of semantic meanings, first they signify one or more senses, and then they refer to things in the outside world. In other words, they have 1. signification and 2. reference.

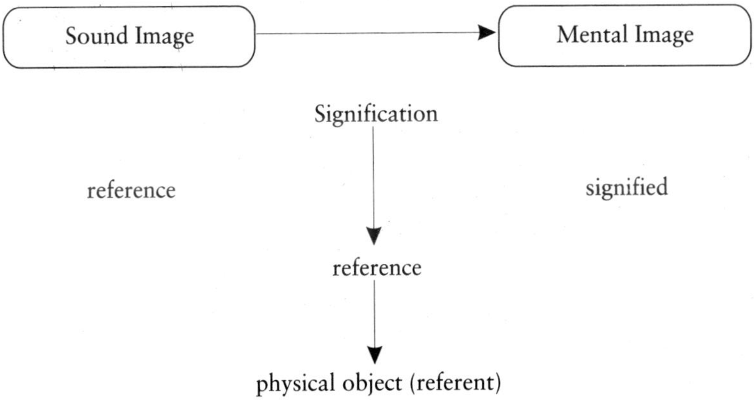

While studying semantics we try to find out the connotative value of the lexical items. The connotative value is again determined by collocation, and, therefore, it may be said that a word is known by the company it keeps. Though 'happy' and 'merry' indicate the same state of mind we say 'Happy New Year', but 'Merry Christmas'. The two words 'happy' and 'merry' are not interchangeable, and therefore, *Merry New Year and *Happy Christmas are not acceptable forms of greetings in English.

Consider the connotations of *slim, skinny, willowy* and *slender* used in the following sentences.

1. Reena has a lovely, slim figure.
2. Tina should eat more, she is much too skinny.
3. She is tall and willowy.
4. The dancer moved her slender body gracefully.

Though both the words *slim* and *skinny* mean thin, *slim* is used approvingly, having a positive connotation, while *skinny* is used disapprovingly implying a negative connotation. Again, *willowy* is not only approving, it is used especially of a woman who is not only thin but is also extremely graceful. *Slender* is used in describing a woman who is thin and delicate in an attractive way.

While using semantics in the stylistic analysis of a text, we should try to find out the correlation between the 'lexical meaning' and the 'sentence meaning' of the lexical items. The lexical meaning of *run* in the sentence 'The boy runs every morning.' is 'moves fast from one place to another, but *run* in the sentence 'He runs a shop near the cinema hall.' does not mean 'moving from one place to another', it means he has a shop near the cinema hall. The meaning relationships of the lexical items, and not the meaning of the individual lexical items are studied in semantics.

2.2.4 Discourse

The analysis of language in use is called 'discourse analysis'. Language serves two functions: **transactional** and **interactional.** According to Browne and Yule (1983) the function which language serves in the expression of content may be called transactional while the function involved in expressing social relations and personal attitudes may be termed as interactional. Transactional language is mainly 'message oriented'. Discourse analysis is interested in the interactional rather than the transactional use of language.

Amol: Have you noticed the man sitting at the gate of the park?

Geeta: Who? You mean that *bloke*?

Geeta's statement is interactional as she used the informal word *bloke* to express her assessment of the man referred to by Amol.

A wide range of syntactic forms may used by a speaker to express the same propositional or factual information, but depending on the context, the speaker chooses a particular syntactic form, and this choice is conditioned by the interactional function of language. Consider the following sentences said by A to B:

A: His father built the house.
The house was built by his father.
It was his father who built the house.
It was the house his father built.
What his father built was the house.
The house, his father built.

Though the same propositional content is expressed in all these sentences, different syntactic forms are used to convey different implicated meaning. A speaker often manipulates the structure of his utterance to focus on the intended meaning he wants to convey. The sentence 'His father built the house.' is the normal way of telling B that someone's father built the house. The second sentence might be the answer to B's question ' What was built by his father—the house or the boundary wall?'

While uttering a sentence, the speaker faces the problem of arranging his words in a particular sequence. How to begin an utterance? Which word or expression should come first? The choice of the appropriate order of words and the selection of the appropriate form of the sentence are very crucial in conveying the intended meaning. The beginning point of an utterance often influences the hearer's interpretation of everything that follows in a particular utterance.

Brown and Yule (1983) use the term 'theme' to refer to the left-most constituent of a sentence and observe that each simple sentence has a theme which is the starting point of an utterance. Everything else that follows the 'theme' is called 'rheme'. In the sentence 'His father built the house' 'His father' is the theme, while in the sentence 'The house was built by his father' 'The house' is the theme. The choice of the theme, therefore, is conditioned by the interactional function of the language. The changing of the thematic structure of an utterance may change the intended meaning of the utterance.

While looking for the 'theme' or the left-most constituent of a sentence it has to be remembered that the theme is not always the grammatical subject. The 'theme' is what the sentence is about, it is immaterial whether it is the grammatical subject or not. It is a stylistic device, not a grammatical category. Consider the following sentences and see how adverbials of locations are thematised.

1. In the Kaziranga national park of Assam you will see the one-horned rhino.
2. On some islands you can enjoy your holidays with a low cost budget.
3. At some airports, you may not get a prepaid taxi.
4. In some countries we have our representatives to welcome you at the airport.

Just as travel brochures thematise locational adverbials, detective novels often thematise time adverbials:

1. Late at night the police officer on duty saw a man slipping through the window.
2. At 8 o'clock in the evening, the car parked in front of the hotel. An hour later a man in his thirties drove away hurriedly.
3. While he was keeping a vigil, his companion rang him.

Various frameworks have been proposed for describing language use in contexts, and the 'speech act theory' of J.L.Austin (1962) needs a special mention in any discussion on stylistics. The speech act theory treats an utterance as an act performed by a speaker in a context with respect to an addressee. Performing a speech act involves performing 1. a locutionary act, the act of producing a recognisable grammatical utterance in the language, and 2. an illocutionary act, the attempt to achieve some communicative purposes. Illocutionary acts are generally classified into the following groups:

1. Representatives
2. Expressives
3. Verdictives
4. Directives
5. Commissives
6. Declarations

Representatives are illocutionary acts that undertake to represent a state of affair such as stating, claiming, describing, telling or suggesting. Expressives are illocutionary acts that express the speaker's psychological attitude towards some state of affairs. Verdictives are illocutionary acts that try to assess, estimate or judge a statement. Directives are illocutionary acts which aim at directing the addressee to do something such as requesting, commanding, and inviting. Commissives are illocutionary acts that commit the speaker to do something like promising or threatening. Declaratives are illocutionary acts that bring about the particular state of affairs they refer to, such as blessing, bidding or arresting. Illocutionary acts are conditioned by the context in which they occur, and a native speaker knows it intuitively how, when, where and by whom they can be performed. Consider the following utterances:

1. What is your age?
2. How old are you?

The degree of formality appropriate to the occasion will prompt the speaker to use either the first utterance or the second.

Austin (1962) pointed out that 'the uttering of the sentence is, or is part of, the doing of an action, which again would not normally be described as saying something'. Consider the following sentences:

1. Could you pass on the salt please?
2. I pronounce you man and wife.

3. I am extremely sorry.

In these sentences, the speaker not only conveys some messages, he also performs the acts of requesting, declaring and apologising. Now, consider the following sentences used by an Assamese speaker:

1. *mai za:ba pa:rimne tumar logot?* (Can I accompany you?)
2. *lagate za:bo pora: za:y neki ba:ru?* (Would it be possible for me to accompany you?)

Both the sentences have the same propositional value, but the second sentence is considered to be more polite than the first sentence. While inviting somebody an Assamese speaker may use either of the following sentences:

1. *tu:mi a:hiba dei.* (Please do come.)
2. *tu:mi naha:koi na:tha:kiba: dei* (Don't stay back, please.)

The second sentence is more persuasive than the first. When does an Assamese speaker use the first and when does he use the second? It depends on the interpersonal function of the language in a particular context.

2.2.5 Context

That there is a difference between the lexical meaning and the sentence meaning has been discussed in the previous section. Consider the following two lines from Yeats' poem *An Irish Airman Foresees His Death*:

> Those that I fight I do not hate,
> Those that I guard I do not love:

So far the English lexicon is concerned, the words *fight* and *guard* and *love* and *hate* are opposed to one another. But in the above mentioned lines these lexical items have lost their opposition to the Irish airman as he finds it impossible to distinguish between loving and hating or guarding and fighting. In other words, the opposition between the lexical items has been neutralised in this particular context.

Consider the following proverbs:

1. A rolling stone gathers no moss.
2. Our parents are our guests. Treat them well.

What does the first proverb imply? A positive meaning or a negative one? According to the *Cambridge Advanced Learner's Dictionary*, 'A rolling stone gathers no moss' means a person who is always travelling and changing jobs and is without any sense of responsibility', therefore, from the traditional point of view a person who moves like a rolling stone has a negative image in society. But in the context of globalization and the job opportunities available in multinational companies, a young person who jumps from one job to another like a rolling stone has a positive image in society. The second proverb may seem quite innocent and reverential in the context of a traditional Indian family. A newly married young man is asking his wife to treat his parents the way a host treats his guests. But think of a nagging wife complaining all the time against her parents-in-law and the young man asking her to tolerate them for a few days more as the guests (his parents) will leave sooner or later. That there is nothing intrinsic in a message is evident in the following utterances:

1. Mother (to her baby on her lap): You naughty boy!
2. Teacher (to a pupil): You naughty boy!

'Naughty' may not always mean naughty, it can be used as a term of endearment. It is the context that makes the meaning explicit. A word, it may be said, is known by the company it keeps.

2.2.6 Syntax

The study of syntax helps us to examine the way words are arranged in speech or writing to make well-formed sequence of words for transmitting a particular message. The sequence of words forms a string and a speaker or a writer manipulates the string to serve his stylistic need according to the context in which he transmits his message. Saussure pointed out that we can look at any string of words as having two axes: a horizontal axis (syntagmatic), along which words combine with other words, and a vertical axis (paradigmatic), along which they interchange with other words.

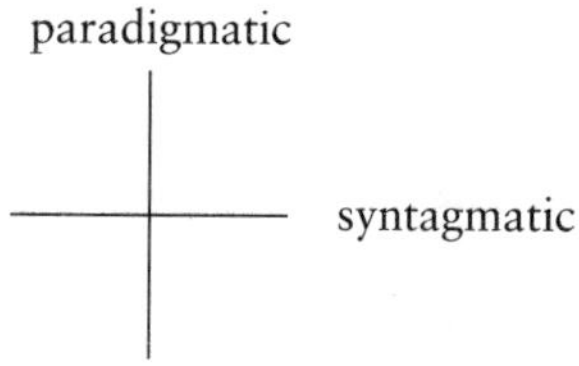

In stylistic analysis, we try to find out how the syntax helps us to understand the communicate value of a text. Consider the following nursery rhyme:

> Tom, Tom, the piper's son
> Stole a pig, and away he ran
> The pig was eat, Tom was beat
> And Tom went howling down the street

In this nursery rhyme, *stealing, running, eating* and *beating* took place one after the other, but Tom's *going down the street* and *howling* occurred simultaneously. The syntax changes according to the meaning of the rhyme.

Syntax also helps us to find out the relation between the form and function of an utterance. Consider the following utterances:

1. Pass the salt.
2. Please pass the salt.
3. Will you pass the salt?
4. Would you pass the salt, please?
5. Can you pass the salt?
6. Could you possibly pass the salt?
7. You couldn't possibly pass the salt, could you?

With each permutation of 'Pass the salt' the degree of politeness increases. Now, consider how the poet in the following lines of *An Irish Airman Foresees his Death* manipulates the strings of words:

a. The years **to come** seemed **a waste of breath**

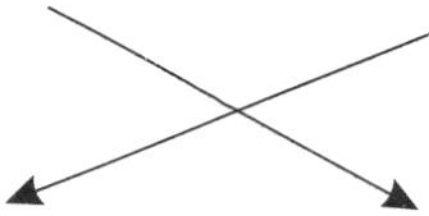

A waste of breath the years **behind**

b. *Those that I fight* **I do not hate,**

Those that I guard *I do not love:*

In a. a waste of breath occurs in the second half of the first sentence, but it occurs in the first half of the second sentence. In b. the first part of the first sentence is related to the last part of the second sentence, and the second part of the first sentence is related to the first part of the second sentence. Is it a mere coincidence or is it due to the stylistic effect that the poet wants to make? The Irish Airman is fighting high up in the sky, and it seems that the movement of the plane has led to a movement of the syntax of the poem.

2.3 SUMMING UP

Stylistics unfolds the relationship between language and its artistic and communicative functions. It helps us to explore creativity in language use for a better appreciation of the message conveyed with the help of language. While studying stylistics we should remember that the mere counting of nouns and verbs of a text or the listing of cohesive devices cannot unearth the stylistic features of a text. A true stylistician uses linguistic as well as extra-linguistic parameters to study a discourse in its proper perspective. The linguistic structure of a discourse is an index of its stylistic function and therefore, the stylistician has to analyse all the linguistic features of the discourse in great details. Sounds, lexis, semantics, discourse patterns, contexts and syntax are some of the stylistic tools generally used by stylisticians to interpret the communicative value of a discourse.

Exercises

1. How does the study of lexis give us valuable clues to the meaning of a discourse?
2. Discuss the basic principles of 'discourse analysis'.
3. What is 'speech act theory'? Discuss the basic tenets of the speech act theory with suitable examples drawn from your own language.
4. Bring out the differences between 'lexical meaning' and 'sentence meaning'.

3

Stylistic Features

3.1 COHESION

Cohesion is an umbrella term for the various ways in which meaning relations in a text are combined intersententially. Cohesion indicates a semantic relation between an element in a text and some other element that is crucial to its interpretation. The two elements, however, may be structurally related or unrelated to each other. Consider the following text:

> When you meet my father tell him to relax.

The element 'him' is directly related to my 'father' semantically as well as structurally. When somebody utters these sentences we understand the implied cohesion even when the two sentences are not structurally related:

> The bus met with an accident. Several passengers were injured.

Cohesion makes its presence felt when the interpretation of any item in a discourse requires making a reference to some other items in the discourse.

In their book *Cohesion in English*, Halliday and Hasan (1976) have given the most comprehensive introduction to cohesion used in a literary discourse and assert that cohesion is 'realised through the lexicogrammatical system' of the language. While some forms of cohesion are realised through the grammar of the text, some are realised through its vocabulary.

> While going to college I met a man. The man was a foreigner.

'A man' of the first sentence becomes 'the man' in the second. As 'the man' refers back to 'a man' it is called an *anaphoric* reference. The anaphoric function of 'the man' gives cohesion to the two sentences.

It's really a difficult subject. I mean stylistics.

The element 'It' refers forward to 'Stylistics' of the second sentence. When an element refers forward to another element it is called a *cataphoric* reference.

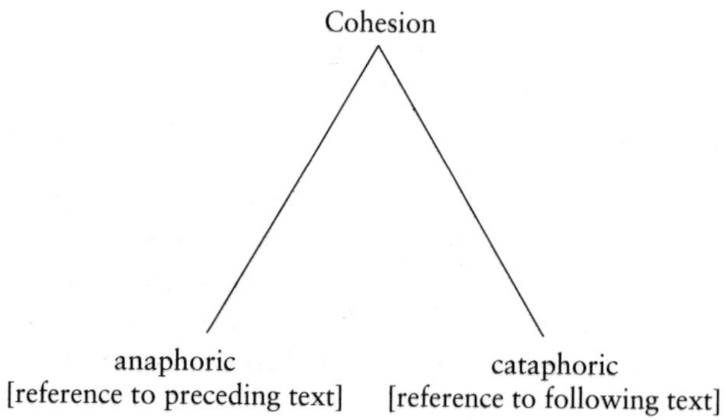

As already pointed out, cohesion is a linguistic means by which sentences are woven together to create a meaningful and intelligible text and a study of the cohesive devices helps us to find out the links between or across sentences. Halliday and Hasan (1976) have discussed quite elaborately various kinds of cross-sentence cohesive links found in texts and they have also drawn up a list of various kinds of cohesive devices. The four basic types of cohesion are:

1. Reference
2. Ellipsis
3. Conjunction
4. Lexical

3.1.1 Reference

A grammatical word in one sentence in association with a word or a phrase is used in another sentence.

Manise invited me to her country. She lives in Thailand.

'She' of the second sentence does not make any sense unless it refers back to 'Manise'. The pronoun 'She' makes an anaphoric reference to 'Manise' of the first sentence. If we read only the first sentence we cannot identify the country as we do not know where Manise is from. As soon as we read the second sentence, the cataphoric reference makes it evident that she is from Thailand.

The reference cohesion includes personal pronouns, regular and possessive demonstratives and the definite article 'the'.

3.1.1.1. Personal Reference

The personal reference means the use of personal pronouns, possessive determiners and possessive pronouns to establish a link to what has been stated earlier.

1. *Reena and Seema* are very intelligent. They always get good marks in maths.
2. *Tina* has left for England. We feel *her* absence very much.
3. *I* could not attend your lecture. The loss is *mine.*
4. *We* are Indians. We are proud of *our* country.

3.1.1.2. Demonstrative Reference

When a speaker identifies the referent by locating his referent on a scale of proximity, either spatial or temporal, like *here, there, now, then* we call it demonstrative reference.

1. *This* is the place where our martyr sacrificed his life.
2. *These* oranges are not for sale. You may buy the other ones.
3. Jim is sitting in the drawing room. You may go *there* if you like.
4. *That* was a nice outing, indeed!
5. *There* seems to be an uneasy relationship between the two friends.
6. We went to Delhi last year. *That* was our first visit to the city.
7. You have wasted your time playing. There is no point in crying *now.*

3.1.1.3. The Definite Article 'the'

The definite article, 'the' functions as a cohesive device when it indicates that the item in question is specific and identifiable.

1. Be careful. *The* road ahead is dangerous.
2. He returned a book but it was not *the* book that I had wanted.
3. The Prime Minister was greeted by *the* journalists who had gone to the airport to meet him.

3.1.2 Ellipsis

Ellipsis is the omission of one or more words from a text, which the hearer or reader can recover or guess from the context. A particular element in a text is sometimes left out as its repetition is felt to be irrelevant. Ellipsis occurs when some shortened or condensed structure is used for the full sequence.

1. You have many books on stylistics. Can you lend me *some?*
2. What's the time by your watch? Sorry, I'm not wearing *one.*

In 1. above 'some' stands for 'some books on stylistics', while in 2. 'one' stands for the'watch'.

Ellipsis may be broadly grouped into three categories: *nominal ellipsis, verbal ellipsis* and *clausal ellipsis*

3.1.2.1 Nominal Ellipsis

When ellipsis occurs within the nominal group it is called nominal ellipsis.

1. The *candidates* are waiting outside. *Both* are full of expectation.
2. Take these *notes* today. I will give you *more* tomorrow.

In 1. 'Both' stands for 'the candidates', while in 2. more implies 'notes'. As the ellipsis occurs in the nominal group it is called nominal ellipsis.

3.1.2.2 Verbal Ellipsis

When an ellipsis occurs within the verbal group it is called *verbal ellipsis.*

1. What are you doing?—Studying.
2. Have you noticed his new car?—No, I haven't.

In 1. 'Studying' stands for 'am studying', in 2. 'haven't' stands for 'haven't noticed'.

3.1.2.3. Clausal Ellipsis

Clausal ellipsis occurs when there is an omission of a whole clause without affecting the communicative value of the message.

1. Jane: The meeting has been postponed.
2. Mary: Why?

In the above dialogue, 'Why' occurring in stands for the clause 'why has it been postponed?' But, Mary does not feel it necessary to reproduce the whole clause, she uses an elliptical form 'Why'.

3.1.3 Conjunctions

When conjunctions are used, usually at the beginning of a sentence in order to establish the logical relationship of the information that follows with the information that has been given before, they are called *cohesive conjunctions.* The clusters of cohesive conjunctions are as follows:

1. Additive (and, or, similarly, in other words etc)
2. Adversative (yet, but, however, rather, on the contrary etc)
3. Causal (so, then, as a result, otherwise etc)
4. Temporal (then, next, first, to sum up etc)
5. Continuation (now, of course, surely, after all etc)

3.1.4 Lexical Cohesion

When repeated uses of the same content words or their synonyms convey a sense of integratedness of a text it is called *lexical cohesion.* Lexical cohesion may be any one of the following types:

3.1.4.1 Simple repetition of a given word:

1. Water, water, everywhere
   Not a drop to drink
2. *My daughter*! O my *ducats*! O *my daughter*!
   Fled with a Christian! O my Christian *ducats*.

3.1.4.2 Use of synonyms or near-synonyms:

1. Bring me my bow of burning gold!
   Bring me my *arrows* of desire!
   Bring me my *spear*! O clouds unfold!
   Bring me my Chariot of fire!

2. Busy old fool, unruly Sun
   Why dost thou thus
   Through *windows*, and through *curtains* call on us?

3.1.4.3 Use of a subordinate, super ordinate or general term to denote a particular entity on a latter occasion.

There was no *furniture* in the room, not even *a chair*.

3.1.4.4 Collocation

Collocation is a kind of lexical cohesion that occurs through the association of lexical items that co-occur regularly. It is the combination of words formed when two or more words are frequently used together arbitrarily.

1. Happy New Year *but* Merry Christmas
2. Hard snow *but* not strong snow

In 1. the words 'happy' and 'merry' have the same lexical meaning, but we cannot interchange 'happy' with 'merry'. *Merry New Year and *Happy Christmas are not acceptable greetings in English. In 2. 'hard and 'snow' collocate, but not 'strong' and 'snow'.

3.2 SPATIO-TEMPORAL REFERENCE

When I get a phone call from Jakarta, the caller introduces himself saying that he is calling from Indonesia. But when some one from Delhi calls me, he introduces himself saying that he is from Delhi, he does not say that say that he is from India. When someone where I live calls me, the caller does not say that he is calling from Guwahati, if he lives at Beltola in Guwahati he will say that he is calling from Beltola. The examples of people making phone calls from Jakarta, Delhi and Guwahati indicate that in any interaction speakers make a conscious decision about what constitutes a relevant and recognisable frame of spatial reference to anchor the communication.

The temporal perspective of the addresser is also quite important for transmitting a message successfully. The writer of a narrative or a speaker initiating a dialogue has to make decisions about what constitutes a relevant frame of temporal reference. A person, for example, asks her colleague: 'When are you retiring?' and the colleague replies, 'September'. The answer 'September' implies that the person is retiring in the month of September of the particular year in which the conversation is taking place. But if he is to retire in 2020 he will not mention the month, he will just say '2020'.

The spatio-temporal perspective of the speaker or the writer is normally anchored with the help of *deictics*. Deictics, originally from the Greek 'deiktos' means able to show directly. They are the orientational features of language, and they locate an utterance or expression in relation to a speaker's or a writer's view point in space and time.

Deictic terms like *this that, here, there* are spatial while the terms *now and then, today* and *tomorrow* are temporal. In English, tense is used to anchor an utterance or a statement from the perspective of the speaker. Tense locates events along an imaginary time line—past, present and future. Temporal references are sometimes embedded in a sentence. We can say:

> I look forward to the coming years.
> But we cannot say:
> *I look forward to the past years.

Similarly we can say :

> Come here soon.
> But we cannot say:
> *Go here soon.

The use of the deictic term *here* after the verb 'go' is not permissible in English. The speaker or the narrator of a discourse always tries to modify the listener's or the reader's awareness by using deictic terms. This also serves the purpose of orientation by establishing a shared universe with the listener or the reader. The *Once upon a time* formula may be cited as an example of orientation with the help of deictic terms. The moment a narrator starts a story with *Once upon a time* the reader realises that it is a fairy tale. Moreover, the use of *Once upon a time* as a feature of orientation anchors the temporal reference of the narrative. In English, a narrator may say

> Once upon a time there was a king named Ashoka.

But a narrator cannot say

*Once upon a time there was an astronaut named Kalpana Chawla

The constraint of the genre of folk tales does not permit the second sentence.

The creation of a shared world between the speaker and the listener or between the narrator and the reader is essential for the transmission of a message.

The use of a common sense geography, spatial and temporal deixis and thematic organisation of a discourse condition the listener's or the reader's awareness and reaction to the message transmitted by the speaker or the narrator. In this paragraph from *Far from the Madding Crowd*, Thomas Hardy uses spatial as well as temporal references to create a shared domain in which the imaginary incident takes place.

> The field he was in this morning sloped to a ridge called Norcombe Hill. Through a spur of this hill ran the highway between Emminster and Chalk-Newton. Casually glancing over the hedge, Oak saw coming down the incline before him an ornamental spring wagon, painted yellow and gaily marked, drawn by two horses, a waggoner walking alongside bearing a whip perpendicularly.

The spatial references to *the ridge*, *a spur* or the *highway* are quite significant as features of orientation as the writer anchors the incident in a particular geographical location; and for a proper appreciation of the narrative the geography presented in the novel plays a very important role. The temporal reference to *in this morning* anchors the plot in time.

By presenting the spatio-temporal background, the speaker or the narrator invites the listener or the reader to participate in the discourse. The degree of the speaker's or the narrator's presence—from complete domination to self-effacement, and the degree of participation solicited by the speaker or the narrator come under the broad term *point of view*. The speaker or the narrator has a linguistic responsibility in creating the right kind of *point of view* necessary for the proper transmission of the message. The decoding of the message is a collaborative venture of the speaker and the listener or the narrator and the reader. The following paragraphs taken from D.H. Lawrence's short story *The Odour of Chrysanthemums* indicates how the narrator conditions the readers' perception by his own point of view.

> The engine whistled as it came into the wide bay of railway lines beside the colliery, where rows of trucks stood in harbour.
>
> Miners, single, trailing and in groups, passed like shadows diverging home. At the edge of the ribbed level of sidings squat a low cottage, three steps down from the cinder track. A large bony vine clutched at the house, as if to claw down the tiled roof. Round the bricked yard grew a few wintry primroses. Beyond, the long garden sloped down to a bush-covered brook course. There were some twiggy apple-trees, winter-crack trees, and ragged cabbages. Beside the path hung dishevelled pink chrysanthemums, like pink cloths hung on bushes. A woman came stooping out of the felt-covered fowl-house, then drew herself erect, having brushed some bits from her white apron.
>
> She was a tall woman of imperious mien, handsome, with definite black eyebrows. Her smooth black hair was parted exactly. For a few moments she stood steadily watching the miners as they passed along the railway; then she turned towards the brook course. Her face was calm and set, her mouth was closed with disillusionment.

By describing the features of the landscape with a photographic fidelity, Lawrence conditions the response of his readers with a sense of immediacy. The spatial references prompt the readers to look at the narrative structure of the story from the point of view of the narrator. A look at the following spatial references indicates the way the narrator invites the readers to share his knowledge of the physical world seen from a spatial perspective. With the help of these spatial references a reader can draw a diagram of the particular area of the colliery referred to by Lawrence.

wide bay of the railway lines
at the edge of the ribbed level of sidings

round the bricked yard
beside the path

the colliery
three steps down from the cinder track
beyond, the long garden

Toolan (1988) who discusses the question of text and time in his book *Narrative; A Critical Linguistic Introduction* says that 'time is inescapably linear and there is an obvious and immediate disruption of any neat co-relation of real time to text time as soon as the narrative involves more than one story-line.' A narrative described in the past tense may be sub-divided into different time frames with reference to the actual time of occurrence. In the following lines of William Blake's poem *The Chimney Sweeper*, though two activities took place in the past they are presented sequentially without any disruption of any co-relation of real time to text time:

> When my mother died I was very young,
> And my father sold me while yet my tongue
> Could scarcely cry "weep! weep! weep! weep!"
> So your chimneys I sweep, and in soot I sleep.

Now, consider this nursery rhyme:

> Humpty Dumpty sat on a wall,
> Humpty Dumpty had a great fall
> All the kings' horses and all the kings' men,
> Could not put Humpty Dumpty together again.

In this nursery rhyme, all the activities took place in the past but the narrator's point of view has structured them with reference to a linear verbal representation of temporality.

Three temporal references made in the nursery rhyme are 'sitting on a wall', 'falling down' and 'the attempts made by the kings' horses and kings' men' without disturbing the linear progression. As all the three activities are noticed one by one by the narrator, and the reader or the listener is also conditioned to view them one by one. The sequence of events narrated in the nursery rhyme and their actual order of presentation in the text are not distorted by the narrator and the children can well visualise the incidents sequentially. But in the following nursery rhyme all the events do not take place one after another:

> Tom, Tom, the piper's son
> Stole a pig and away he ran;
> The pig was eat
> And Tom was beat
> And Tom went howling down the street.

While *stealing*, *eating* and *beating* follow one another, *running* and *howling* go together. Though the two activities are referred to in the last line of the rhyme, they are presented as a single unit by the poet and this indicates that a choice can be made from among the various points of view from which the narrative elements are presented.

Let us now consider how Hardy uses temporal reference in the beginning of *The Return of the Native* and *Tess of the d'Urbervilles*.

> A Saturday afternoon in November was approaching the time of twilight, and the vast tract of unenclosed wild known as Edgon Heath embrowned itself moment by moment.
>
> (*The Return of the Native*)

> On an evening in the latter part of May a middle-aged man was walking homeward from Shaston to the village of Marlott, ...
>
> (*Tess of the d'Urbervilles*)

3.3 SPEECH AND THOUGHT PRESENTATION

While narrating an incident, we usually report the events from our own point of view, the main events, in the third or first person and in the simple past or present tense. But in order to save the narrative from being monotonous we often report what the characters said or thought and try to reproduce their speeches as faithfully as possible. An author has a number of choices in the manner the thought and speech of the characters are displayed. He can use the actual words uttered by the characters without any modification and can create an impression that the characters are speaking in our presence. He can just refer to the nature of the speech made by the characters without quoting the actual words. The nature of the speech and thought presentation depends on the degree of the involvement of the narrator. Is the narrator totally neutral? Does he intervene, what is the magnitude of this intervention? Whose voice do we listen to when we go through the words uttered by a character? The author's or the character's? Can we listen to both the voices—the author's as well as that of the character?

Leech and Short (1981) have classified speech and thought presentation in fiction into five categories. They are:

Narrative Report of Speech Act/Narrative Report of Thought Act	NRSA/NRTA
Indirect Speech/ Indirect Thought	IS/IT
Free Indirect Speech/Free Indirect Thought	FIS/FIT
Direct Speech/Direct Thought	DS/DT
Free Direct Speech/ Free Direct Thought	FDS/FDT

3.3.1 The Presentation of Speech

1. The Narrative Report of Speech Act (NRSA)

   The narrative report of speech act (NRSA) is more indirect than indirect speech. Here the narrator does not reproduce the actual words uttered by the person whose speech is being reported. When a writer reports the speech made by a person without actually quoting the words uttered by him, we see the event entirely from the writer's perspective. Consider the following report published in a newspaper:

   > The Prime Minister regretted the protectionist policies of the West.

   This sentence is based on the reporter's assessment of the speech act performed by the Prime Minister. The reader has no access to the actual words uttered by the Prime Minister. In NRSA, the report is shown entirely from the narrator's perspective.

2. Direct Speech (DS)

   In Direct Speech (DS), the words uttered by the speaker are quoted within inverted commas. A narrator uses the direct speech to report verbatim what a character said in a particular context.

"I hope we will be able to convince Germany to look at this issue for mutual benefit," Dr Singh said.

3. Free Direct Speech (FDS)

In Direct Speech, the narrator reports what the character uttered in a particular context. But in Free Direct Speech (FDS) the characters speak directly without the intermediacy of the narrator, and, consequently the reporting clause is omitted in the presentation of such a speech.

> She cried and threw her arms around his neck saying: "O Bob! Bob! What am I to do? What am I to do at all?"—DS
>
> "Polly! Polly!"—FDS
>
> "Yes, mamma?"—FDS
>
> "Come down, dear. Mr. Doran wants to speak to you."—FDS

4. Indirect Speech (IS)

In Indirect Speech (IS), the words of the speaker are reproduced in the third person with a reporting verb and the speech is presented from the point of view of the narrator.

> Prime Minister Manmohan Singh remarked that Germany would respond positively to India's energy requirements by extending support to India's energy programme.—IS
>
> She said that she would be happy to stand by him.—IS

In Indirect Speech, the reported speech is always dependent on the reporting verb and the narrator intervenes as an interpreter between the readers and the person whose speech he reports. Unlike Direct Speech, Indirect Speech does not reproduce the speech verbatim.

5. Free Indirect Speech (FIS)

Free Indirect Speech (FIS) occupies a place between Direct Speech and Indirect Speech. In Free Indirect Speech, the reporting verb is omitted but the function of the 'tense' is similar to that of its function in Indirect Speech. Carter (1982) has captured the unique characteristics of Free Indirect Speech saying, "With a free indirect speech, or FIS, a kind of fusion takes place between authorial and character view point in which the shape and texture of the character's voice can be preserved without any loss of the narrator's objective interpretation of events." He elaborates his observation with the help of the following example:

> He stopped and said to himself, 'Is that the car I saw yesterday?'—DS
>
> He stopped and asked himself if that was the car he had seen there the day before.—IS
>
> He stopped. Was that the car he had seen yesterday?'—FIS

Free Indirect Speech is neither a verbatim reproduction of the original speech nor is it a mere indirect rendering of the original. Leech and Short (1981) remark that Free Indirect Speech involves some kind of a distancing effect in the sense that due to the intervention of the authorial voice between the reader and the words of the character, the reader is distanced from the character's words.

3.3.2 The Presentation of Thought

Just as the speech can be presented as NRSA, IS, FIS, DS, FDS the thoughts of the characters can also be presented as NETA, IT, FIT, DT, FDT

1. Narrative Report of Thought Act (NRTA)

   Here the writer does not reproduce the thought of the character; he simply records the character's thought process.

   He longed for a change. (NRTA)

   She wondered what she should do. (NRT)

   She felt sure she would win. (NRTA)

2. Direct Thought (DT)

   Here the thought of the character is reproduced verbatim by the narrator.

   "I need a change," he thought. (DT)

   "What should I do?" she wondered. (DT)

3. Free Direct Thought

   Here the thought of the character is presented directly without the intermediacy of the narrator, and, consequently, the reporting clause is omitted in presenting the thought.

   I need a change. (DT)

   What should I do? (DT)

4. Indirect Thought (IT)

   Here the thought of the character is reported in the third person with a reporting verb.

   He thought that he needed a change. (IT)

   She wondered what she should do then. (IT)

5. Free Indirect Thought (FIT)

   Free Indirect Thought occupies a place between Direct Thought and Indirect Thought, As Leech and Short point out, "The FIT version differs from that of DT by virtue of the backshift of the tense and the conversion of the first person pronoun to the third person (indirect features) and also by the absence of a reporting clause and the retention of the interrogative form and question mark (direct features)."

   What should she do now? (FIT)

   What reparation would he make? (FIT)

While the norm for the presentation of speech is DS, the norm for the presentation of thought is IT. Again, while FIS distances the readers from the characters, FIT brings the readers nearer to the inner world of the characters. The relative position of the different modes of thought presentation as shown by Leech and Short (1981) is given below:

1. By using IS and NRSA, the narrator indicates that the actual words uttered by the characters are not of great importance.
2. By using DS, the narrator indicates that the actual words uttered by a character are important.
3. When a narrator uses DT, he assumes the role of an omniscient

narrator who can render the thoughts of his characters in the first person.

4. When a narrator uses IT, he is just a reporter of the inner world of his characters. He seems to be a detached onlooker.
5. When a narrator uses FIT, he intrudes into the inner world of his characters, there is a fusion between the thought of the characters and that of the narrator.

3.4 SUMMING UP

A study of the cohesive devices, the spatio-temporal references and the pattern of speech and thought presentation found in a text helps us in appreciating a message in its totality. These stylistic features help us in sharpening our intuitive responses to a text; they act as passwords for unlocking the web of words of a literary or a non-literary text. The following checklist based on Leech and Short (1981) and Short (1996) has been prepared to help students in their stylistic interpretation of texts.

3.4.1 Lexis

a. Examine the nature of the lexical items used in the text. Are they descriptive or evaluative, denotative or connotative?
b. Do the words form lexical chains? If yes, how do they help you in relating them to the main ideas contained in the text?
c. Are there any unusual words that do not conform to the general pattern of the words used in the text? If yes, can you account for the unusual occurrences? How does the unusual use of some words help the writer to convey a special meaning?
d. Is there frequent use of the first person pronominal?
e. Look at the formal and the informal categories of the words.
f. Look at the verbs. How frequently do they occur? Are they verbs of action or verbs of perception ? Is there any correlation between the use of verbs and the general theme of the text.
g. What is the frequency of the use of adverbs? Are they adverbs of location or time adverbials. How do they helping you in capturing the spatio-temporal references of the text?

3.4.2 Grammar

a. Consider the sentence types. Are they simple, complex or compound? Consider the clauses, if any. Is the use of a particular sentence type conditioned by the meaning of the text.

b. Is there unusual placement of clauses in a sentence. If any, does it contribute to the general message of the text?

3.4.3 Cohesion and Coherence

a. Look for anaphoric and cataphoric references used in the text.

b. Look for deictic terms, ellipsis and repetitions and find out how they help you in capturing the meaning of the message.

c. Consider the nature of the speech presentation in the text. Is there any predominance of a particular style of speech presentation? If yes, how is it related to the thought content of the text?

Exercises

1. What is cohesion? Distinguish between 'anaphoric' and 'cataphoric' cohesions.
2. What do you mean by ellipsis? Discuss various types of ellipsis with suitable examples quoted from literary texts.
3. What is deixis? How do deitic terms help an author in providing spatio-temporal references in a discourse?
4. Discuss the commonly used techniques of thought and speech presentations in novels.
5. Read this speech by Satan in Milton's *Paradise Lost* Book I and find out the cohesive devices and the spatio-temporal references made in the speech.

> Hail,horrors ! hail
> Infernal world! and thou profoundest Hell,
> Receive thy new possessor—one who brings
> A mind not to be changed by place or time.
> The mind is its own place, and in itself
> Can make a heaven of Hell, a Hell of Heaven

What matter where, if I be still the same,
And what I should be, all but less than he
Whom thunder hath made greater? Here at least
We shall be free, the Almighty hath not built
Here for his envy, will not drive us hence;
Here we may reign secure, and, in my choice,
To reign is worth ambition, though in hell:
Better to reign in Hell than serve in Heaven.

[ll. 250–263]

4

Appreciating Poetry

4.1 LITERARY STYLISTIC ANALYSIS

The main objective of stylistics has been to try to account objectively for the meaning of a text, and this objective is achieved by systematically analysing the language of the text. Stylistics, it has to be reiterated, is based on the assumption that a rigorous and systematic study of the language of a text enables a reader to appreciate its meaning in its totality. But this basic assumption is often questioned by critics of stylistics. Gower (1986:139) opposes any literary stylistic analysis of literature as he considers it to be too mechanistic and cerebral in operation, and maintains that instead of helping readers appreciate literature, a stylistic analysis actually impedes the whole process of reading and appreciating literature. According to Gower, when a text is put 'under a microscope' and the readers' attention is drawn to the analytical procedures, aesthetic qualities of the text are diminished and the readers who 'work under such laboratory conditions' fail to appreciate the emotional appeal of the text. He feels that when a poem is taken apart for analysis, the analyst fails to recognise the spirit of the poem which is expressed in its totality and not in its part.

Gower's criticism of the use of literary stylistics in the study of literature is difficult to accept, because the analysis of the different parts of a literary text following a literary stylistic model is never an end in itself. The purpose of 'putting a text under a microscope' is to formulate the reader's literary sensitivity in a systematic objective level, and to enhance the appreciation of the aesthetic qualities of the text. Carter, et al (1989) have very convincingly pointed out how a literary stylistic approach enhances the literary experience of the readers. It is, no doubt, very easy to eulogise the ideals of responsive enjoyment and imaginative participation in literature, but it is very difficult to translate them into action in the true sense of the term. Literary stylistic analysis provides the readers with the necessary tools to understand the 'aesthetic qualities' of a text by sensitising the readers to the intricacies of literature.

4.2 A Stylistic Analysis of *The Darkling Thrush*

Lexis is often regarded as a starting point for the study of the nature of language, and a study of the ways lexical items are patterned in a poem gives the reader valuable clues to the meaning of the poem. Lexical items, their semantic incompatibilities and unusual collocations show the readers how a poet uses language to create a particular effect. Let us take a look at the first two stanzas of Thomas Hardy's *The Darkling Thrush.*

I leant upon a coppice gate
When Frost was spectre-grey,
And Winter's dregs made desolate
The weakening eye of day.
The tangled bine-stems scored the sky
Like strings of broken lyres,
And all mankind that haunted nigh
Had sought their household fires.

The land's sharp features seemed to be
The Century's corpse outleant.
His crypt the cloudy canopy,
The wind his death-lament.
The ancient pulse of germ and birth
Was shrunken hard and dry,
And every spirit upon earth
Seemed fervourless as I

In these two stanzas a number of lexical items build a picture of decay, desolation and death leading to a sense of negation. A string of lexical items is formed by words referring to the world of death: *spectre*, *string of broken lyres*, *haunted*, *corpse*, *crypt*, *death-lament*, and *spirit*. Another set of lexical items is formed by words referring to decay and desolation: *dreg*, *desolate*, *weakening eye*, *broken lyres*, *shrunken*, *fervourless*. The sense of negation generated in the first two stanzas infects some of the lexical items of the third stanza also.

At once a voice arose among
        The bleak twigs overhead
In a full-hearted evensong
        Of joy illimited;
An aged thrush, frail, gaunt, and small,
        In blast-beruffled plume,
Had chosen thus to fling his soul
        Upon the growing gloom.

Lexical items such as, *bleak, aged, frail, gaunt, small, blast beruffled, gloom* intensify the negative world view of the poet and act as cohesive devices. The use of lexical items connoting negation is almost absent in the fourth stanza. Only two lexical items *little* and *unaware* carry on the sense of negation in this stanza:

So little cause for carolings
        Of such ecstatic sound
Was written on terrestrial things
        Afar or nigh around,
That I could think there trembled through
        His happy good-night air
Some blessed Hope, whereof he knew
        And I was unaware.

As the third and fourth stanzas project a quasi-religious hope, a string of lexical items refers to religious joy: *evensong, fling his soul, carolings, blessed songs, ecstatic sounds, happy good-night air*.

In order to interpret any text we should not only discuss intra-textual collocation of language items, but also the code from which the language items derive their original meaning. For the interpretation of any text, both the contextual meaning and the referential meaning are equally important. The collocation of *winter* and *dregs*, *mankind* and *haunted* are rather unusual. Dregs are bits of matter, which sink to the bottom of a container or a bottle of liquid, but in order to suggest something exhausted and discarded, the poet has juxtaposed *winter* and *dregs*. The refuse found at the close of winter is like the dregs of an empty bottle. Again, while mankind dwells or lives, ghosts or spirits haunt. But the lexical incompatibility of *mankind* and *haunted* has been neutralised by lexical patterning along with the equivalence of form and rhythm.

> The tangled bine-stems scored the sky
> Like strings of broken lyres,
> And all mankind that haunted nigh
> Had sought their household fires.

The lexical items *mankind, lyres, household fires* create a false sense of comfort and harmony: mankind had sought household fires, which has in all probability been extinguished now; a lyre with broken strings implies death (the picture of broken lyres on funeral cards). The first and the second lines of the above stanza have four feet each, the second and the fourth lines have three feet each; all the feet are iambic, *sky* rhymes with *nigh, lyres* rhymes with *fires*. In a normal language code mankind is /+ physical/, but the creatures which haunt this world are supposed to be /- physical/. In line 15, the inhabitants of the earth are referred to as spirits, a lexical item which is also /-physical/. Thus, death and desolation have robbed mankind of its earthly physical existence, and there is no distinction between the living and the dead.

The lexical items *features* and *corpse* connote human beings, but in order to convey the all-pervasive theme of death, the poet uses them in association with land and century. Time (*century*), place (*land*), and actors (*mankind*)—all are dead and gone, the dirge is sung by the wind and not by the poet who is as fervourless as the spirits haunting the graveyard of mankind.

Lexical items also create a notion of disorder, disharmony and discord. *Tangled bine stems* suggests things being scratched and twisted. While music connotes harmony, strings of broken lyres connote disharmony. The metaphysical connection between the landscape and the corpse suggests a perplexing and confused world view. The unusual collocation of *winter* and *dregs*, *mankind* and *haunted* creates a sense of tension and indicates a dislocation of sensibility. The sense of opposition and tension is also generated by the following lexical items: *winter* and *household fires*; *germ*, *birth* and *hard*, *dry*, *joy* and *gloom*; *afar* and *nigh*, *could think* and *knew*. It is significant to note that while thinking is a rational activity, knowing is intuitive awareness. The bird's intuitive awareness of *Some blessed hope* is more basic than the poet's cold logic.

The patterning of lexical items also projects an individual's isolation and detachment from the collective strength of society. In *I leant upon a coppice gate* the lexical item *I* refers to a single person, *coppice* is a small group of trees growing very close to each other; *dregs*, a collection of solid particles along with the last drops of liquid; *the weakening eye of day* is a solitary entity; *features* are all the parts of a person's face; the *corpse* is a single entity; and *a solitary voice* arose among the *twigs* overhead. Singularity in the background of plurality brings out the theme of isolation quite prominently.

Besides lexis, **deixis**, the formal device for indicating how the speaker is related to what he refers to, can also be 'a point of entry' for literary interpretation. In *The Darkling Thrush,* deictic terms *the*, *a*, *an* and *some* indicate the panorama of disorder and the poet's inability to respond to the positive aspects of life. The definite determiner *the* is used to identify the lexical items which intensify the growing gloom:

the weakening eyes of day
the tangled bine stems
the sky
the land's sharp features
the century's corpse
the cloudy canopy
the wind
the ancient pulse
the bleak twigs
the growing gloom

The thrush and its song are presented with indefinite determiners:

a voice arose
a full-hearted even song

an aged thrush
some blessed Hope

The poet's uncertainty about the meaning of the bird's song is thus reflected even by the use of the deictic terms.

The use of *a* in *I leant upon a coppice* gate is a deviant use of a deictic term in this poem. The fact that the poet leant upon a gate and observed the growing gloom is enough to identify the gate as a particular one. But the poet chooses to keep a sense of indefiniteness in identifying it as *a* gate, not *the* gate. In this connection, it is significant to note that *copse*, a synonym of *coppice* is phonetically almost similar to *corpse*. The poet leant upon *a copse* gate; it could be the 'corpse' gate, the gate leading to the world of the dead.

In the first stanza we have verbs connoting physical action: *leant, made, scored, haunted, sought*. But in the second stanza *outleant* is used as a post-modifier and *shrunken* is in the passive voice. The verb of perception *seemed* occurs twice in the second stanza, and it indicates that while the first stanza is an objective portrayal of nature, the second stanza is subjective in its perception. The third stanza again uses verbs connoting physical action: *arose*, *chosen* and *fling*. In the fourth stanza, verbs of action as well as verbs of perception co-exist: *was written*, *think*, *trembled*, *knew*, and *was unaware*. The poet does not maintain the pattern of the use of verbs in the last stanza; he jumbles up the verbs of action and the verbs of perception in this stanza. The sense of disorder is thus intensified by the patterning of these verbs.

Stanza I	verbs connoting physical action	objective
Stanza II	verb of perception	subjective
Stanza III	verbs of action	objective
Stanza IV	verbs of action + verbs of perception	objective+ subjective

The study of the nominal groups used in the poem sheds light on the construction of meaning in the texture of the poem. The normal pattern of the structures of nominal groups found in the poem is DMH, that is, determiner, modifier and headword:

A coppice gate	DMH
The weakening eye	DMH
The tangled bine stems	DMH
Their household fires	DMH

All the headwords except *the sky*, *land*, *century*, *wind* and *mankind* have modifiers. Mankind, however, is not grouped with the *sky, land, century or wind*, because it is modified by a post- modifier *that haunted nigh*. The elemental things and concepts are presented as they are without any modifier—*the sky*, *land*, *century* and *wind*. The equivalence of form used in the presentation of mankind and the thrush intensifies the theme of contrast and conflict. Both mankind and the thrush have post-modifiers, and the past perfect tense is used in presenting their activities:

a. And all mankind *that haunted nigh*	post-modifier
Had sought their household fires	past tense
b. An aged thrush, *frail, gaunt and small*	
In blast-beruffled plume	post-modifier
Had chosen thus to fling his soul	past tense

The first two stanzas are composed of two sentences each, but the last two stanzas are composed of one sentence each. The first two stanzas are mostly descriptive; the camera seems to move from one object to the other. The third stanza is both descriptive and meditative, and then in the fourth stanza it is completely meditative. That the fourth stanza is completely meditative, is evident even in the structure of the sentence used in the stanza. The whole stanza is a complex sentence which can be found in any prose writing. First, read the lines as presented by the poet in the poem and then read it as a piece of prose writing.

So little cause for carolings
        Of such ecstatic sound
Was written on terrestrial things
        Afar or nigh around,
That I could think there trembled through

His happy good-night air
Some blessed Hope, where he knew
And I was unaware

'So little cause for carolings of such ecstatic sound was written on terrestrial things afar or nigh around that I could think there trembled through his happy good-night air some blessed Hope where of he knew and I was unaware.' The use of a number of subordinate clauses indicates the poet's dependence on cold logic.

The poem is written in the past tense, and besides past tense markers we have past participles as well: *leant, made, tangled, scored, broke, haunted, sought, seemed, outleant, shrunken, arose, chosen, was written, could think, trembled, knew, was unaware.* In the background of these eighteen past tense markers and past participles, there are only two present participles: *weakening* and *glowing*. These two present participles imply a sense of continuity, a frightening feeling of the imminent catastrophe.

The poem starts with an assertion: 'I leant upon a coppice gate' and the nominal groups are well connected with the verbs. In the second stanza, the use of the verb *seemed* implies lack of certainty. Moreover, the third and the fourth lines of the second stanza are without any verb, and the absence of any verb indicates an absence of a cause-effect relation. In the third stanza, the thrush is introduced in an indirect manner:

A voice arose

A full-throated evensong

An aged thrush

First, it is a mere voice, then it is an evensong, and it is only when we have read half of the stanza we are told that it is an aged thrush. While the speaker, *the bine stems, mankind* and the *crypt* are introduced in a quite straightforward manner; the thrush gets a different treatment. The use of the modal *could* in the last stanza also indicates the poet's sense of uncertainty, and in spite of the *full-hearted evensong* of the thrush, the poet fails to find any ray of hope, and admits his inability to take part in the bird's *happy good-night air.*

4.2.1 Summing up

While reading Hardy's *The Darkling Thrush* literary critics are often moved by its superb aesthetic qualities and the note of pessimism pervading the poem. But is it possible to account for the 'aesthetic qualities' or the 'note of pessimism' without putting the poem under a microscope? By applying the tools like lexical items, deictics, semantic incompatibilities, deviation, lexical and grammatical cohesion and verb patterns we have tried to appreciate the poem in its true perspective. Far from diminishing our appreciation of the beauty of the poem the stylistic analysis heightens our appreciation of the artistic quality of the poem.

4.3 A STYLISTIC ANALYSIS OF *A MARTIAN SENDS A POSTCARD HOME*

A Martian Sends a Postcard Home by Craig Raine is a poem of thirty-four lines written from the point of view of an imaginary visitor coming to the earth from Mars. The tone of the poem is highly imaginative, the riddles and the metaphors used in the poem pose a challenge to the reader. In this poem, the visiting Martian tries to make a sense of an alien world. Let us try to find out how the poet uses language to bring out the point of view of the Martian with a different consciousness.

> Caxtons are mechanical birds with many wings
> and some are treasured for their markings—
>
> They cause the eyes to melt
> or the body to shriek without pain.
>
> I have never seen one fly but
> sometimes they perch on the hand.
>
> Mist is when the sky is tired of flight
> and rests its soft machine on ground:
>
> then the world is dim and bookish
> like engravings under the tissue paper.
>
> Rain is when the earth is television.
> It has the property of making colours darker.
>
> Model T is a room with the lock inside—
> a key is turned to free the world

for movement, so quick there is a film
to watch for anything missed.

But time is tied to the wrist
or kept in a box, ticking with impatience.

In homes, a haunted apparatus sleeps,
that snores when you pick it up.

If the ghost cries, they carry it
to their lips and soothe it to sleep

with sounds. And yet, they wake it up
deliberately, by tickling with a finger.

Only the young are allowed to suffer
openly. Adults go to a punishment room

with water but nothing to eat.
They lock the door and suffer the noises

alone. No one is exempt
and everyone's pain has a different smell.

At night, when all the colours die,
they hide in pairs

and read about themselves—
in colour, with eyelids shut.

The poet uses several riddles in this poem to describe what a Martian observes when he comes to earth. The first stanza is about books. Caxton was the first English printer and therefore, books are called caxtons by the Martian. Mechanical birds with wings refer to the pages of a book. The Martian remarks that the books are treasured for their markings implying that if a person enjoys reading a book he will treasure it. Books are referred to in the next four stanzas. In the sixth stanza Raine talks about fog. "Rain is when the earth is television" is a wonderful metaphor. In the seventh and eighth stanzas the Martian talks about a car. 'Model T is a room with the lock inside'. The driver has to go inside the car and he needs a key to turn the car on and off and to lock it. A watch or a clock is described in the ninth stanza. A haunted apparatus, as it seemed to the Martian, is described in great details in the next three stanzas. An ordinary object like a telephone gets a highly poetic description in the tenth, eleventh and the twelfth stanzas. A mundane affair like that of going to a lavatory is described rather ingeniously in the next three stanzas. The last two stanzas are the culmination of the superb poetic vision of Craig Raine. 'Men read about themselves in colour with their eyelids shut'.

A detailed stylistic analysis of the stanzas 10, 11, 12 is presented in this chapter. The lexical groupings are as follows:

haunted	sleeps	pick it up
ghost	snores	carry it
	cries	soothe it
	wake it up	

The word 'telephone' is not mentioned in the poem, it is just an apparatus and is referred to as '*it*' time and again:

when you pick *it* up
they carry *it*
soothe *it* to sleep
they wake *it* up

The foregrounding of 'home' in *In homes* serves the purpose of orientation, and the poem remains incomprehensible until we correlate *homes* and *it*. *They* and *their* also play significant roles in the poem:

they carry it
their lips
they wake it up

The use of deictic terms also plays an important role in the poem:

a haunted apparatus
the ghost
with *a* finger

The lexical items taken from the world of reality are not used in the sense of their meanings as ordinarily perceived, they are used in a different context and their semantic values also undergo a sea change. While reading Craig's poems, a reader has to play a co-creative role and he has to form a coherent picture of the world presented in the poem with a particular reference to the world of the text. The spatio-temporal reference presented in the text also serves the purpose of orientation of the readers:

In homes, a haunted apparatus sleeps

The foregrounding of the words 'In homes' specifies the setting of the text in a very familiar background, but this specification is rather an illusion, the readers' expectation is shattered in the Noun Phrase that follows:

A haunted apparatus sleeps

The grammatical deviation of the first line is also quite significant. The normal word order of the first line should have been

a haunted apparatus sleeps in homes

but to highlight the importance of the location the poet has used deviation. The contrast with the world of reality and a twisting of the normal world view are effectively done by the unusual collocation of the lexical items.

home	+human
haunted apparatus	–human

The expression *If the ghost cries* stands for *when the ghost cries* and the expression *by tickling with a finger* stand for *when they tickle it with a finger*. The use of the cohesive devices is also quite significant in the poem. The *haunted apparatus* has a cataphoric reference to *that* and *it* of the sentence *That snores when you pick it up* but the word *they* has neither an anaphoric nor a cataphoric reference. Naturally, the readers fail to identify *they* as the inhabitants of the earth. Though *they* comes after *ghosts*, it has no anaphoric reference to ghosts. The identity of *they* is crucial for an understanding of the poem, the poet does not make it obvious, the appeal of the poem would have been lost if the poet had stated everything explicitly. The poem is not just about a *telephone*; it is about a *recreated telephone* from the point of view of a Martian visitor.

Widdowson (1975) refers to the importance of studying the code and the context of language used in a literary discourse. Following Widdowson we may study the lexical items used in the poem. The lexical item *apparatus* may be distinguished from the lexical item *snores* in that its semantic specification in the code of language would include/ - inanimate/ whereas the specification for *snores* would be/+

animate/. The two lexical items are not, therefore, semantically compatible in the code of the language. An inanimate object like an apparatus cannot sleep and snore but the poet has deviated from the established code to create a new world where inanimate objects can sleep and snore. It also helps the poet to create a distancing effect and a world of make belief where impossible things may happen. Such a twisting of the language code is in conformity with the point of view of a visitor from Mars who seems to have a new vision and a new diction.

The poem has a note of interpersonal communication and it gives the poem a note of informality:

> that snores when *you* pick it up

The absence of a nominal group identifying *they* or *there* is also characteristic of a spoken discourse. Stylistically, it is an example of endophoric reference. The identity of *they* remains clouded in mystery due to this endophoric use of *they*. A note on informality coupled with a note of immediacy makes the poem apparently incomprehensible.

4.3.1 Summing up

It is often thought that Raine's poetry is incomprehensible and 'requires a reader's or listener's guide before approaching the work' (Booth, 1985). But by using the tools of stylistics—lexical items, collocation, foregrounding and deictic terms we can understand the apparently incomprehensible message of his poem. The stylistic analysis presented in this section points out the fact that while reading Raine's poetry a reader has to play a pro-creative role to decipher the meaning. The apparently incoherent picture of the world presented in the poem appears coherent and logical only when it is studied from the point of view of stylistics.

4.4 A STYLISTIC INTERPRETATION OF *THE BUTCHER*

Craig Raine's poem *The Butcher* is a realistic portrayal of a butcher who goes on with his regular business dispassionately. He cuts animals into pieces of meat, sells sausages, bacon, pork and chicken while his apron gets dirty with blood stains. As a professional butcher he kills animals with impunity. The customers who gather at his shop are equally unconcerned about the killing of animals.

The poem points out the ambivalent attitude of the butcher and his customers. The slaughter of innocent animals is routine work for the butcher who is eager to satisfy the demands of his customers. He smokes, woos his customers, sells sausages, bacon and mince and drinks his tea with the spoon held back. His blood-stained, striped apron or the pound notes soiled with the blood of the slaughtered animals do not repulse him. The compulsion of his profession has robbed him of his finer sensibilities. The poem is as follows:

> Surrounded by sausages, the butcher stands
> smoking a pencil like Isambard Kingdom Brunel
>
> He duels with himself and woos his women customers,
> offering thin coiled coral necklaces of mince,
>
> heart lame-ed from the fridge, a leg of pork
> like a nasty bouquet, pound notes printed with blood.
>
> He knows all about nudity–the slap and trickle
> of blood, chickens stripped to their aertex vests.
>
> He rips the gauge from dead balletic pigs,
> and makes the bacon slicer swish its legs.
>
> How the customers laugh! His striped apron
> gets as dirty as the mattress in a brothel......
>
> At 10, he drinks his tea with the spoon held back,
> and the Great Eastern goes straight to the bottom.

A preliminary reading of the poem draws our attention to a lexical chain created by the following lexical items:

sausages	butcher
pork	chickens
pigs	bacon
apron	

These lexical items show us a picture of a typical butcher who sells meat and is engrossed in his business. But Raine is not interested in presenting the picture of an ordinary butcher; he is interested in presenting *the real* as *the unreal*. His objective is to make the common picture uncommon and this prompts him to startle the reader with unusual collocations and present the butcher in a new light. The following lexical chain gives a new twist to the picture of the butcher:

nudity

stripped

balletic

mattress in a brothel

The dehumanizing nature of his job brings a negative sensation in the poem and this negative sensation is heightened by the lexical items referring to *a brothel*. The butcher's shop and the brothel come from two incompatible registers of the language, the code of the language does not allow the juxtaposition of these lexical items, but the poet has identified them as similar places. The slaughterhouse of animals and the slaughterhouse of human dignity are equally degrading. The use of the word '*blood*' in the following lines is noteworthy:

like a nasty bouquet, pound notes printed with *blood*

of *blood*, chickens stripped to their aertex vests.

Though the poem is about a *butcher*, he is introduced in the *rheme,* not as the *theme* of the first line:

Surrounded by sausages, *the butcher* stands

But though the butcher gets a secondary importance in the first line of the poem, he regains his position in the following lines:

He duels with himself

He knows all about nudity

He rips the gauge

In the last stanza, however, he is relegated to a secondary position; the temporal reference gets the thematic importance:

At 10, *he* drinks his tea with spoon held back,

The description given in the poem is from the butcher's point of view:

his women customers
His striped apron
he drinks *his* tea

The verbs of action are quite prominent in the poem:

> the butcher *stands*
> He *duels*
> he *rips*
> and *makes* the bacon
> he *drinks*
> and the Great Eastern *goes* straight to bottom

Though the poem is about an ordinary butcher in his normal surroundings, it is basically a commentary on the sordid human tragedy that engulfs human sensibilities. Though the physical settings have a vividness that tries to endow the poem with a sense of reality, there is a sense of instability at the psychological plane. The butcher, his customers, pigs, pork, chickens and sausages hang together precariously in the general drama of annihilation of human sensibility. The cruelty and callousness of customers visiting a butcher's shop, the unconcerned attitude of the customers, the impersonal approach of the butcher present a grotesque and macabre picture in the poem.

The lexical item *duel* in the code of the language means a formal fight between two people in which they use guns, swords or other weapons in order to settle a quarrel. In the poem the butcher duels with himself as though he has a split personality. The formal word *duel* does not collocate with the word *woo*, but the poet has juxtaposed the two words to indicate the absurdity of the situation. A necklace is a piece of jewellery which is worn round the neck, usually by women. The butcher *woos* his women customers with *thin coiled coral necklaces* of beef which has been cut into very small pieces. Coral is a hard substance that forms in the sea from the skeletons of very small animals; therefore, the reference to the *coral necklace of mince* is a typical example of the juxtaposition of apparently unrelated lexical items. The following imageries are not only unusual, they are startling too:

> necklaces of mince
> a leg of pork like a nasty bouquet
> pound notes printed with blood
> dirty as the mattress in a brothel

4.4.1 Summing up

The study of the lexical items and their unusual collocation helps us to grasp the total effect of the bizarre imageries presented in the poem. The far-fetched imageries have a distancing effect and they bring out the grotesque atmosphere in its totality. Raine is not afraid of presenting the slaughterhouse in a very dispassionate manner and the stark realism of the poem prompts us to look at the familiar scene from a new perspective.

4.5 A STYLISTICS ANALYSIS OF *HOME THEY BROUGHT HER WARRIOR DEAD*

Tennyson's *Home they brought her warrior dead* portrays the reaction of a wife who is devastated by the shock and trauma of the death of her husband who is killed in battle. Let us read the poem and try to use some of the tools of stylistic analysis to gauge the magnitude of the wife's emotions as conveyed by the poet.

Home they brought her warrior dead
    She nor swoon'd nor utter'd cry
All her maidens, watching said,
    She must weep or she will die.

Then they praised him, soft and slow
    Call'd him worthy to be loved,
Truest friend and noblest foe,
    Yet she neither spoke nor moved.

Stole a maiden from her place,
    Lightly to the warrior stept,
Took the face-cloth from the face,
    Yet she neither moved or wept.

Rose a nurse of ninety years,
    Set his child upon her knee—
Like summer tempest came her tears—
    Sweet my child, I live for thee.

As the poem centers round the wife of the dead warrior a number of lexical items refer to the warrior's wife. Consider the following lexical chain:

Her warrior
She
Her maidens
She
She
She
She
Her knee
Her tears

The following lexical chain refers to the dead warrior:

Warrior
Him
Him
Truest friend
Noblest foe
Warrior
The face

An examination of the lexical items reveals the sources of cohesion of a text and it helps us to discover the recurrent themes or images in a text. The lexical choice made by a writer or a speaker is intimately associated with the choice of the subject matter. In this poem, there is a concentration of lexical items referring to the wife of the dead warrior. In the first four lines 'she' is used five times. The repeated use of the same lexical item has an auditory as well as a visual effect on the reader or the listener.

On seeing the dead body of her husband, the lady was so terribly grief-stricken and benumbed that she neither fainted nor cried out. The absence of any visible expression of grief made the maidens attending her worried and apprehensive of an imminent danger to her life. The repeated use of lexical items relating to the lady indicates that the poet wants to put the primary focus on the lady who was the centre of attention and concern at the moment. Though the lexical item *warrior* occurs in the very first line of the poem the warrior is not the focus of attention. He is *her* warrior, and therefore, the point of reference is the lady, not her dead husband. After focusing on the wife and projecting her prominently in the first stanza, the camera moves on to the dead body of her husband and focuses on him in the second stanza and, therefore, we have lexical items like *him*, *friend* and *foe* in the second stanza.

> they praised him
> Call'd him worthy
> Truest friend
> noblest foe

A study of the lexical items indicates that there is a pattern in the presentation of the maidens too. In the third and the fifth lines, we get a collective presentation of the maidens, in the ninth and the thirteenth lines it is an individual presentation. While the collective effort of the maidens did not yield the desired result, the individual effort of a particular nurse achieved the objective.

All her maidens — line 3
↓
They — line 5
↓
A maiden — line 9
↓
A nurse — line 13

The activities of the maidens also form a lexical chain. The verbs of action used to refer to the activities performed by the maidens are as follows:

> watching
> Stole
> Said
> Stept
> Praised
> Took
> Call'd
> set

Out of these activities, some are done collectively and some individually. They *watched* the lady, *said* that she must weep and *praised* the dead warrior collectively. At the individual level, a maiden *stole* from her place, *stept* to the dead warrior, *took* the face cloth from his face, a nurse *rose* and *set* his child on the knees of the grief -stricken wife.

The verbs used in the poem present a sense of contrast and opposition in the poem. While some verbs are +movement others are –movement. Verbs in column A are + movement while those in column B are –movement.

A (+ movement)	B (– movement)
brought Stole Took stept Set came	swoon'd utter'd cry watching said weep die praised Call'd

In the first two stanzas of the poem, the maidens also did not show any sign of movement. They *watched*, they *said*, they *praised* him, they *called* him worthy to be loved. But in the third stanza of the poem there is a sudden shift, a maiden *stole* from her place, *went* to the dead body and *removed* the face cloth from the warrior's face. In the fourth stanza, a ninety-year-old nurse gets up and *sets* the child on the knees of the wife of the dead warrior. Thus there is an opposition between the first two stanzas and the last two stanzas of the poem.

Two lexical items connoting action and movement are foregrounded in the third and the fourth stanzas of the poem. Instead of saying 'A maiden stole from her place' the poet says *Stole a maiden from her place*. Similarly, instead of saying 'A nurse of ninety years rose' the poet says *Rose a nurse of ninety years*. By foregrounding *Stole* and *Rose*, the poet focuses on the importance of these two verbs of action in the overall atmosphere of inaction. Similarly, by placing *Stole* and *Rose* in a thematic position the poet has highlighted the implication of these two lexical items.

The lexical items help us to visualise two planes on which the drama unfolds. These two planes may be called horizontal and vertical. The dead body was lying horizontally in the presence of the wife and the maidens who were sitting on a horizontal plane. Sitting around the dead body, the maidens were watching, praising and calling the dead warrior worthy to be loved. These activities taking place at the horizontal level are followed by activities showing vertical direction. A maiden stood up (vertical movement) and she was followed by an old nurse who rose from her seat, again showing vertical movement.

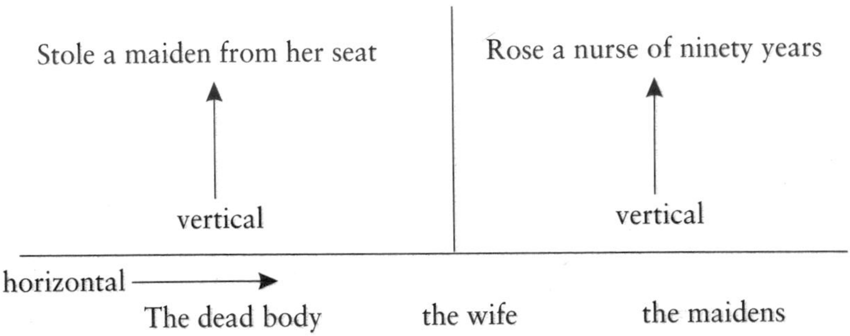

The syntax of the poem also heightens the tension generated in the poem. The last line of the second stanza and the last line of the third stanza bring out the sense of helplessness and despair of the maidens.

Yet she neither spoke nor moved line 8

Yet she neither moved nor wept line 12

That all their efforts had failed is highlighted by placing *Yet she neither* in thematic positions in these two lines. It is, however, significant to note that this syntactical pattern is not used by the poet in the first stanza. The second line of the first stanza 'Neither did she swoon nor uttered cry' is semantically similar to the eighth and the twelfth lines, but is deviant syntactically from these two lines. The normal syntactic pattern of the second line of the first stanza should be 'Neither did she swoon nor uttered cry', but the line deviates from the normal English sentence pattern to show the unusual reaction of the grief-stricken wife.

4.5.1 Summing Up

The recurrent themes of the poem are presented in a highly cohesive manner with the help of the lexical chain used in the poem. The stylistic analysis presented in this section also reveals the importance of the syntax used by a poet in his poem. The analysis of the poem has also tried to bring home the fact that there is a correlation between the deviant syntax and the grief-stricken deviant behaviour of the wife of the dead warrior.

4.6 A STYLISTIC ANALYSIS OF *TO THE SKYLARK*

In his poem *To a Skylark*, Wordsworth addresses the bird as an ethereal being who soars high up in the sky invoking a spirit of joy and happiness. The bird's song creates a world of absolute bliss and the poet is moved by its melodious strain. The poet wonders how the skylark could forsake its nest to soar high up in the sky. Listening to the bird's song and observing its movement, the poet tries to find out the reason behind the happiness that is reflected in the song of this small singing bird. The poet thinks that though the bird soars high up in the sky, it is not oblivious to its earthly moorings. The love for its near and dear ones prompts the bird to soar in the sky singing such a melodious strain.

> ETHEREAL minstrel! pilgrim of the sky!
> Dost thou despise the earth where cares abound?
> Or, while the wings aspire, are heart and eye
> Both with thy nest upon the dewy ground?
> Thy nest which thou canst drop into at will,
> Those quivering wings composed, that music still!
>
> To the last point of vision, and beyond
> Mount, daring warbler!—that love-prompted strain
> —'Twixt thee and thine a never-failing bond—
> Thrills not the less the bosom of the plain:

Yet might'st thou seem, proud privilege! to sing
All independent of the leafy Spring

Leave to the nightingale her shady wood;
A privacy of glorious light is thine;
Whence thou dost pour upon the world a flood
Of harmony, with instinct more divine;
Type of the wise who soar, but never roam;
True to the kindred points of Heaven and home.

Here, it is worthwhile to note that though the poem is addressed to a skylark, the name of the bird is not used in the poem. The skylark has been addressed in the second person and the words *thou, thy, thee* and *thine* are used quite liberally in the poem to create a world of interpersonal communication.

Dost thou despise the earth where cares abound?
Both with thy nest upon the dewy ground
Thy nest which thou canst drop into at will,

'Twixt thee and thine a never failing bond—
Yet might'st thou seem, proud privilege! To sing

A privacy of glorious light is thine,
Whence thou dost pour upon the world a flood

Why does the poet use the words *thou, thy, thee* and *thine* instead of you and your? The lexical meaning of thou, thy, thee and thine indicates that the poet has used them as words denoting divinity. The words *ethereal, divine* and *heaven* also belong to the same lexicon. The skylark is addressed as a pilgrim of the sky as the poet visualises it as a person who makes a journey to a holy place for a religious purpose. The word *pilgrim, thou, thy, thee, thine, ethereal, divine* and *heaven* have a religious association and the cumulative effect of these words is distinctly felt in the poem. The skylark is not an ordinary bird of the mundane world. It is transported to a higher level and is eulogised as a holy spirit. The sense of complete happiness brought out by the song of the skylark prompts the poet to invoke an ethereal spirit that blurs the distinction between the wood and the sky, the earth and the heaven and the real and the unreal. While reading the poem we notice that the poet is interested in finding out answers to two vital questions:

1. Dost thou despise the earth where cares abound?
2. Or while the wings aspire, are heart and eyes
   Both with thy nest upon the dewy ground?

In the first question the poet asks the skylark whether it dislikes the earth full of cares and anxieties. The poet wonders if the bird soars high up in the sky just to escape the harrowing experience of passing its days in the midst of the miseries of earthly life. In other words, the poet wants to find out whether the bird wants to forsake the earth with its pain and sorrow in search of a better life in the open sky.

In the second question the poet asks the bird whether it has its heart on the ground and looks fixed on its nest upon the dewy ground even when it soars high up in the sky. The poet seems to be very keen in finding out the nature of the bird's sense of attachment to its earthly moorings. With a pointed reference to the *dewy ground* the poet asks the bird if it goes on maintaining a visual as well as a psychological contact with its nest left behind on the ground enveloped by sorrows, miseries and tears.

The skylark is a unifying agent between the two worlds—the world that is full of care and the world of glorious light and bliss. The sense of contrast between these two worlds has been very effectively captured with the help of some lexical items related to the two opposing worlds. The following lexical items refer to the hard world of reality:

earth
earthly
nest
dewy ground
bosom of the plain
shady wood
home

The world to which the skylark aspires after is represented by the following words:

sky
the last point of vision
the glorious light
heaven

The verbs used in the poem also enhance the sense of contrast and opposition between the two worlds. The verbs

despise
canst drop
leave
roam

are related to the earth while

aspire
mount
soar

are related to the world sought after by the skylark. It is pertinent to note that while *roaming* means wandering or travelling horizontally, *soaring* means going up vertically. The horizontal image contrasts with the vertical image and intensifies the sense of contrast and opposition conveyed in the poem.

After the initial doubts about the skylark's motivation, the poet imagines that the music of the bird is prompted by its love for the nest and the near and dear ones left behind on the inhospitable earth. The *love prompted strain* of the skylark pours upon the world a sense of harmony and unifies the two realms. The bird's movements as depicted in the poem add to the central theme. The *wings* of the skylark quiver as it flies and soars high in the sky but the eyes remain fixed to the ground and the concern for its near and dear ones remains fresh in its *heart*. The physical distance does not snap the visual link between the bird and the nest. The bird is far away from the nest on the physical plane but it is very much connected to its nest psychologically. Though the wings create a distancing effect, the *heart* and the *eye* neutralise it.

Words related to music and musicians are used extensively in the poem. Words like

Minstrel	music
Warbler strain	sing

invoke the world of music that enthralls both the earth and the sky. That the poet notices some divine piety in the music of the skylark is evident in the following two lines:

> Whence thou dost pour upon the world a flood
> Of harmony, with instinct more divine,

The poet thinks that divine blessings inspire the skylark to pour out its heart in a melodious strain. In order to highlight the extraordinary quality of the song of the skylark, the poet draws a comparison between the skylark and the nightingale and asserts that the skylark's inspiration is *more divine* than that of the nightingale. While the domain of the nightingale is *the shady wood* of the spring, the skylark encompasses the whole universe. The skylark sings in the ethereal height where the glorious light of the sun illuminates the whole sky and it is indeed his great privilege to reach such a height inaccessible to others.

Eulogising the skylark the poet calls the bird kindred of the wise. In spite of their spiritual enlightenment, wise men do not ignore the ordinary duties of life. They adjust their spiritual quest with their earthly existence. Similarly, the skylark also strikes a balance between its earthly moorings and the voyage to the last point of vision.

> Type of the wise, who soar, but never roam—
> True to the kindred point of Heaven and Home.

Wise men are guided by a vision, they strive towards a particular goal and therefore, the question of roaming has no place in their life. The skylark is prompted by a vision and the urge for attaining the ultimate goal prevents it from roaming on the earth, it soars higher and higher.

4.6.1 Summing up

The stylistic analysis of the poem indicates that lexical items have been used quite judiciously by the poet to present the two worlds—the world of care and anxiety and the world of glorious light and bliss. The horizontal and the vertical world view are also very poignantly presented by the poet with the help of lexical items. The syntactical equivalence of the last two lines of the poem balances the horizontal and the vertical axis.

Exercises

1. Following the model of the stylistic analysis of the poems presented in this chapter attempt a stylistic analysis of the following poem:

To Daffodils

Fair Daffodils, we weep to see
You haste away so soon.
As yet the early-rising sun
Has not attain'd his noon
Stay, Stay
Until the hasting day
Has run
But to the evensong
And, having pray'd together, we
Will go with you along
We have short time to stay, as you,
We have as short a spring;
As quick a growth to meet decay,
As you, or anything.
We die
As your hours do, and dry
Away
Like to the summer's rain;
Or as the pearls of morning due
Nee'er to be found again.

While analysing the poem , find out the lexical items which invoke the sense of negation. Consider the şignificance of the visual imageries: *early rising sun, summer's rain, pearls of morning dew*. Consider the structure of the poem. Is there any correlation between the theme and the structure of the poem?

2. Read the following song from Robert Browning's *Pippa Passes* and write a note on cohesion with examples drawn from the song:

    The year's at the spring
    And day's at the morn;
    Morning's at seven;
    The hill side's dew-pearled;
    The lark's on the wing;
    The snail's on the thorn:
    God's in his heaven—
    All's right with the world!

   (Notice the use of a series of lexical items referring to time: year, spring, day, morn, morning, seven. Lark and snail are linked by semantic likeness, both are animals. You may also take into consideration the the syntax of the poem. Except lines 4 and 8, each line has a syntactical similarity. Can you relate it to the theme of the song?)

3. Write a stylistic analysis of *La Belle Dame sans Merci* taking into account a. the choices in vocabulary, b. links between words, c. the overlap of words, d. personal pronouns, e. sentence linkage, f. tense and g. clause structure. After identifying all these features try to relate them to the meaning of the poem.

La Belle Dame sans Merci

"O what can ail the, knight-at-arms,
        Alone and palely loitering?
The sedge is wither'd from the lake,
        And no birds sing.

"O what can ail thee, kinight-at-arms,
        So haggard and so woe-begone?

The squirrel's granary is full,
          And the harvest's done.

I see a lily on thy brow
          With anguish moist and fever dew;
And on thy cheek a fading rose
          Fast withereth too.

"I met a lady in the meads,
          Full beautiful—a faery's child;
Her hair was long, her foot was light
          And her eyes were wild.

"I made a garland for her head,
          And bracelets too, and fragrant zone;
She look'd at me as she did love,
          And made sweet moan.

"I set her on my pacing steed,
          And nothing else saw all day long,
For sidelong would she bend and sing
          A faery's song.

"She found me roots of relish sweet,
          And honey wild and manna dew;
And sure in language strange she said,
          'I love thee true!'

"She took me to her elfin grot,
          And there she wept and sigh'd full sore;
And there I shut her wild, wild eyes
          With kisses four.

"And there she lullèd me asleep,
          And there I dream'd – Ah! Woe betide!
The latest dream I ever dream'd
          On the cold hill side.

"I saw pale kings and princes too,
          Pale warriors, death-pale were they all;

Who cried- 'La belle Dame san Merci
Hath thee in thrall!'

I saw their starv'd lips in the gloam
With horrid warning gapèd wide,
And there I shut her wild, wild eyes
On the cold hill's side.

"And this is why I sojourn here
Alone and palely; loitering;
Though the sedge is wither'd from the lake,
And no birds sing."

5

Stylistic Analysis of Extracts from a Short Story

5.1 FROM *MOTHER AND DAUGHTER*

The purpose of this chapter is to show how extracts chosen from short stories can be analysed with the help of stylistic tools. The first four paragraphs of Lawrence's short story *Mother and Daughter* constitute a single cohesive unit, and hence, these paragraphs are analysed from the point of view of stylistics.

The study of a literary text involves three elements: an intuitive response to the text, an investigation into its textual pattern, and an identification of the stylistic features that support the intuition and demonstrate the patterning. Again, there are two structural planes in a literary text: the plane of articulation and the plane of information. The plane of articulation of a short story normally includes elements like setting, perspective, and development of the plot. The elements of characterisation, symbolism or the creation of an environment are included in the plane of information. In any literary text, these two structural planes are interlocked, and in order to decode the message of a story, we have to interpret the interlocking of these two structural planes embedded in a story.

While reading Lawrence's *Mother and Daughter*, the reader gets the impression that the story is about the antipathy between women and men, and it is the mother's antipathy to men that ultimately forces the daughter to obey her mother. With the help of an analysis of the plane of articulation and the plane of information, this intuitive feeling may be substantiated at an objective level.

5.2 SETTING

Just as the story begins and ends with Virginia, this short text also begins and ends with Virginia. In the first four paragraphs of the story, the three characters—the mother, the daughter, and Henry—seem to be involved in a power game, who is going to control whom? The positioning of the three characters follows a pattern and the symmetrical presentation of the characters heightens the confrontational attitude of the two women embedded in the text.

The first paragraph introduces the two protagonists. The first sentence introduces Virginia, the third introduces Rachael Bodoin, her mother, and the second maintains a balance between the two and keeps them apart. There are symmetrical sequences for the positioning of the two women and the man. In some sequences only the two women are shown on the screen, again, in some sequences Virginia and Henry are presented, the mother is relegated to the background. Keeping in view these sequences, we may divide the second paragraph into four sections. The first section begins with 'Now' and ends with 'several times'. The mother and the daughter are seen together, they are 'more like a married couple than 'mother and daughter'. Out of the four sentences of this section, three sentences have 'They' as their 'themes'. The structure of this section is as follows:

a. mother and daughter

   They

   They

   They

   The second section starts with 'Virginia' and ends with mother, and presents Henry caught in between them. The structure is:

b. Virginia

   Henry

   Her mother

c. Mrs Bodoin

   Henry

   His mother-in-law and Virginia

The third section starts with Virginia and ends with 'parental authority'. The structure is:

d. Virginia
   her mother

The fourth section begins with Virginia and ends with 'My daughter Virginia'. The structure is:

e. Virginia
   her mother
f. Virginia
   Henry
   Mrs Bodoin

The third paragraph may also be divided into four sections. The first section begins with 'The second reason' and ends with 'question'. In this section, Virginia and Henry are shown in two sequences:

g. Virginia
   Henry
h. Virginia
   Henry

The second section begins with 'Vinny' and ends with 'Henry', who is again placed between the two female protagonists. It is significant to note that as the intensity of dislike increases in this section, the positioning of the female protagonists also changes, and both Virginia and her mother stand together on the either side of their target. The structure is:

i. Vinny
   Mrs Bodoin
   Henry
   Vinny
   Her mother

The third section of this paragraph begins with 'she' and ends with 'vanity', and projects Virginia and Henry only, her mother is relegated to the background, 'often as far back as Paris or Biarritz'. The structure is:

j. she
   he

The fourth section begins with 'women' and ends with 'knowing it', and presents the two women bent on wringing 'the neck of the man they think they are loving with all their hearts'. The structure is:

k. women vs. man

In the fourth paragraph Henry backs out and saves his life by extricating himself from the clutches of the two women. In this paragraph he is not in between the female protagonists, he comes out of their clutches. The structure is:

l. Henry

   an old witch

   a young, spellbound witch

Virginia and her mother stand apart in the first paragraph, at the end of the fourth paragraph they come together and Henry 'couldn't see her (Virginia) apart from her mother'. This last sequence also reverses the ordering of the sequence (k) as the structure of this sequence may be presented as:

m. man vs. women

The analysis of the structure of these four paragraphs indicates that there are discernible phases of development in the story, and the theme of antagonism is embedded in the very structure of the paragraphs, and the relationship of the characters is reflected in the typography of the text.

The story is set against the background of a family, and hence, there is a chain of lexical items connoting family relationships: *her mother, husband, mother and daughter, separation, married couple, his mother-in-law, family loyalty, parental authority, daughter, a wife, inherit, her mother's money,* Vinny felt they were *married.*

Temporal references occur in the text almost like a motif. The incident takes place in a sequence of time, and the reader is frequently reminded of the passage of time. Time has taken its toll on both mother and daughter, who are growing old. Virginia earns seven hundred and fifty pounds *a year*, and it is *already* something. Her mother lived in the capitals of Europe *since* the effacement of her husband. Mother and daughter had *some years* of separation, and *now*, in course of *time*, they have become more like a married couple than mother and daughter. They parted *several times* and Virginia is *now* thirty. She lived with Henry for *four years* and *then* Henry left her. When her mother egged her on she had to obey her. She had *long* thrown parental authority to the winds. Henry knew *when* he was being squashed, and Mrs. Bodoin *always* corrected him when he called Virginia Vinny. Virginia was *already* earning four hundred and fifty at the age of *twenty-four*, while Henry earned about twelve pounds *per annum*. Henry thought that Mrs Bodoin would live *forever*, and he lived with Vinny for *two years* in the married sense of the word. Virginia's mother was *always* at the background, often as far back as Paris. Virginia *never* realised that in spirit she too sat on Henry. She could not resist her mother's influence because women, very *often* hypnotise one another, and *in the end* Henry backed out.

The story is told in the simple past tense, but Lawrence often uses the past perfect to portray episodes in a flashback. Lawrence creates an imagined time stream as a dimension of the narrative world, and we can visualise episodes taking place in a sequence. Rachael Bodoin *had lived* in the capitals of Europe, the mother and daughter *had lived* together and parted, for four years Virginia *had been* as good as married. Henry *had writhed* horribly, Virginia *had long thrown* parental authority to the winds, and Henry *had realised* that he would find it hard to earn more.

5.1.2 The actors

Lawrence presents his characters as an omniscient narrator. As Virginia is the central character of the story, all the characters are identified with reference to her. Virginia and her mother are introduced differently. Virginia's description is impersonal, and the emphasis is on her public image, she is an officer in a government department. In the first paragraph no reference is made to her position in the family, and the first sentence does not tell us whether she is the mother or the daughter. Rachael Bodoin is introduced as Virginia's mother, and the reference to the effacement of a 'never very important husband' gives us a glimpse into her domineering personality. Thus, her character portrayal is personal, and the emphasis is on her private image. She is a mother; besides, she is the wife of an effaced husband. She is also referred to as Henry's mother-in-law. Virginia is portrayed in her professional background; her mother is rooted in the family background.

It is significant to note that her mother resents her being called *Vinny*. Henry calls her *Vinny*, which is more personal and informal, but her mother calls her Virginia. Mrs Bodoin is repeatedly referred to as *her mother* (ten times in the four paragraphs), but Virginia is never referred to as *her daughter*. While Mrs Bodoin is referred to as *his mother-in-law*, Virginia is never referred to as *his wife*. Once the writer says 'she had been as good as married to Henry Lubbock', on another occasion he says 'Vinny felt they were married'. While Virginia is just *daughter*, Mrs Bodoin is *mother, her mother, his mother-in-law*, and she had a 'never very important *husband*' before the beginning of the story.

The physical description of the mother and the daughter also differs significantly. Mrs Bodoin *had the health and muscular equipment of the Sphinx*, Virginia had an *elfish face*. While the mother was an *old witch* with *muscles like the Sphinx*, the daughter was a *young spellbound witch, lavish, elfish and weak*.

In the first four paragraphs, Virginia's age is mentioned twice, but no mention is made of her mother's age. Virginia was now *thirty*, and at the age of *twenty-four* she was already earning four hundred and fifty ponds.

Lawrence is very specific in stating Virginia's financial position, but her mother's financial position is stated approximately. Virginia had a good job in a certain government office, and she 'held a responsible position, and earned, to imitate Balzac and be precise about it, *seven hundred and fifty pounds* a year', (italics added) her mother had an income of *about* six hundred a year. The process of identification and the establishment of the relation between the mother and daughter is as follows:

Rachael Bodoin
Her mother
Mrs Bodoin
Rachael
She
His mother-in-law
Virginia Bodoin
Virginia
She
Vinny

Henry Lubbock is first introduced in relation to Virginia as 'she had been as good as married' to him. He is also identified as a 'spoilt young man'. In consonance with the pattern of stating the financial status of characters, Lawrence mentions that Henry had a 'sorry two hundred and fifty', and managed to earn 'about twelve hundred pounds per annum'. He is portrayed as a helpless victim in the hands of the two female protagonists.

So Henry had withered horribly
His mother-in-law sitting on him tight
When he was being squashed
Spread her skirts and calmly set on Henry
She promptly and mischievously sat on him too
Being simply reduced to nothingness
(Virginia) who ate his marrow

Though the two women tried to pin him down Henry had *masculine* vitality, and he did not 'like having his neck wrung'. Hence, in the end he backs out of the relationship.

Besides lexical items, syntactical structures also help in the characterisation. That Virginia was unable to resist her mother's control is expressed with the help of the following syntactical structures:

When her mother egged her on she couldn't help
Virginia had to rush wickedly
She could no more have helped it

The antagonism between Mrs Bodoin and Henry and their opposing personalities are reflected in the following structures:

> He could not stand her mother
> Her mother could not stand him

Virginia's psychological paralysis, and her lack of initiative is reflected in the following repetition of the same structure:

> And *she never realised* the funny little grin
> *She never realised* that in spirit she promptly...

5.1.3 Environment

Lexical items used here create a sense of a lack of specificity and precision. The mother and daughter were more like a married couple, each was a little nervous, Virginia was as good as married to Henry, and she was her mother's accomplice in a helpless sort of family loyalty. The definite article 'the' is sparingly used in the text. Rachael Bodoin had a never very important husband, after some years of virtual separation the mother and daughter once more thought of settling down. Henry was a rather spoilt young man, and anybody whom Mrs Bodoin could not stand she managed to sit on. She was an old witch, and her daughter was a young spellbound witch. Marriage, in the true sense of the term, eludes Virginia, and lexical items create a world of her make-belief. For four years, she had been as good as married to Henry who lived with Virginia in the married sense of the word, and she felt they were married.

The question of marriage is linked with money, and lexical items having an association with money form a chain. Virginia earned seven hundred and fifty pounds, her mother had an income of about six hundred a year, Virginia had not a sou of her own, and Henry had a sorry two hundred and fifty. Henry managed to earn about twelve pounds per annum, he would find it hard to earn more, and Vinny would inherit her mother's money.

Lawrence often comments on the activities of the characters and evaluates their worth and, therefore, some of the lexical items are evaluative rather than descriptive. Virginia had a good job, and held a responsible position. Her mother had never had a very important husband. The mother and daughter had a virtual separation, they were more like a married couple, and they knew one another very well, and each was a little nervous of the other. The daughter did not look like marrying, for years she had been as good as married to Henry who was rather a spoilt young man. Virginia obeyed her mother in a helpless sort of family loyalty; though she did not really want to sit on Henry she could not help it. Her mother had a strange *female* power over Virginia, and the daughter had to rush wickedly and gleefully. Henry called Virginia Vinny to the superlative disgust of her mother. Henry had a sorry two hundred and fifty and earned twelve hundred pounds a year by his *precious* music. Virginia never realized the *funny* little grin that came on her *elfish* face. While Virginia was a young spellbound witch, *lavish*, *elfish* and *weak*, her mother was an *old* witch with muscle *like the Sphinx*.

The manoeuvering of the mother and daughter has been very vividly described with the help of adverbs:

> She managed to sit on *disastrously*.
>
> Virginia had to rush *wickedly* and *gleefully*.

The intensity of their manoeuvering forced Henry to writhe horribly. In the background of negative adverbs like *disastrously*, *wickedly* and *horribly* the neutral adverb '*gently*' in 'they proceed gently to wring the neck of the man' looks ominous.

Words and the sequence of words are often repeated, and the frequent occurrences of such repetitions imply a dull and monotonous life lived by an unmarried woman and her widowed mother. It seems that the mother and her daughter might have used these words and expressions themselves time and again: *her mother had power over her, a strange female power, her mother had another, much subtler form of domination, female and thrilling*. Both these statements could be joined together, but Lawrence keeps them apart to create a sense of moving in a circle. It seems that Lawrence has foregrounded repetitions as a stylistic device. It evokes an atmosphere of stale familiarity and a lack of direction.

> *Her mother* couldn't stand him.

The fact that Henry forsook Virginia is repeated three times in the extract. It seems that Virginia went on ruminating about her break up with Henry:

> Then Henry *let her down.*
> His reason for *going back on Vinny.*
> In the end Henry *backed out.*

5.1.4 Summing Up

With his superb stylistic touch, Lawrence has intensified the magnitude of the theme of confrontation. From a story of a confrontation between Henry and Virginia and her mother, it becomes a story of a confrontation between a man and his women pursuers who want to captivate 'the man they think they are loving with all their hearts'. The transition from Virginia and her mother to women in general takes place very smoothly, 'her mother had power over her, a strange female power'—'And she never realised'—'For they are hypnotised'—'Women hypnotised one another, without knowing it'. Virginia was hypnotised and spellbound. She not only spoilt the man, but also ate his marrow. Henry, spoilt and vanquished, backed out and saved his life.

Exercises

1. Read the following extract from Jane Austen's *Mansfield Park* and analyse it with the help of the stylistic features discussed in the analysis of the opening paragraphs of *Mother and Daughter:*

   About thirty years ago, Miss Maria Ward, of Huntingdon, with only seven thousand pounds, had the good luck to captivate Sir Thomas Bertram, of Mansfield Park, in the country of Northampton, and be thereby raised to the rank of a baronet's lady, with all the comforts and consequences of a handsome house and large income. All Huntingdon exclaimed on the greatness of the match, and her uncle, the lawyer himself, allowed her to be at least three hundred pounds short of any equitable claim to it. She had two sisters to be benefitted by her elevation; and such of their acquaintance as thought Miss Ward and Miss Frances quite as handsome as Miss Maria, did not scruple to predict their marrying with almost equal advantage. But there certainly are not so many men of large fortune in the world as there are pretty women to deserve them. Miss Ward, at the end of a half a dozen years, found herself obliged to be attached to the Reverend Mr Norris, a friend of her brother-in-law, with hardly any private fortune... they began their career of conjugal felicity with very little less than a thousand a year.

(How does the novelist depict a *mercenary* society? How does she present the characteters? Consider the character description after each name. You may also consider the point of view of the narrator. Do you notice the changing perspectives of the narrative? Try to find out the authorial voice and the voice of the characters presented in the passage.)

2. Read the following opening paragraphs of *A Tale of Two Cities* and try to find out the theme of contrast and antagonism embedded in the language of the text:

It was the best of times, it was the worst of times, it was the age of wisdom, it was the age of foolishness, it was the epoch of belief, it was the epoch of incredulity, it was the season of Light, it was the season of Darkness, it was the spring of hope, it was the winter of despair, we had everything before us, we had nothing before us, we were all going direct to Heaven, we were all going direct the other way—in short, the period was so far like the present period, that some of its noisiest authorities insisted on its being received, for good or for evil, in the superlative degree of comparisons only.

There were a king with a large jaw, and a queen with a plain face, on the throne of England, there were a king with a large jaw and a queen with a fair face , on the throne of France. In both countries it was clearer than crystal to the Lords of the State preserves of loaves and fishes, that things in general were settled for ever.

(Look at the lexical chain and the collocation of words. Do you notice any difference between the narrative style of the first paragraph and that of the second paragraph? Consider the spatio-temporal references of the text and try to relate it to the theme of opposition hinted at in the narrative.)

6

Stylistic Analysis of a Short Story

6.1 *THE FLY IN THE OINTMENT*

While the previous chapter presented a stylistic analysis of an extract of a short story, this chapter presents a stylistic analysis of two short stories, one by V.S. Pritchet and another by James Joyce. The analysis of Pritchet's *The Fly in the Ointment* is primarily based on Labov's model of oral narratives, that of Joyce has been done with the help of the stylistic tools presented in Chapter 2.

6.1.1 The Structure of the Narrative

Like other genres of literature, short stories also comprise specific structures, and an enquiry into the structure of the narrative of a story helps us to appreciate its literary meaning. Research into narrative structure has pointed out that there are three main components in a well-formed narrative: a. setting, b. complication and c. resolution and the present chapter makes a stylistic analysis of Pritchet's *The Fly in the Ointment* from the point of view of the narrative structure of the story. But before embarking on a discussion on the narrative structure it is worthwhile to have a look at the seminal work of William Labov, the American sociolinguist.

6.1.2 Labov's model

On the basis of his analyses of the oral stories of young African American men in New York, William Labov suggested that a fully formed oral narrative of personal experience generally consists of the following six elements.

1. Abstract: what, in a nutshell, is this story about?
2. Orientation: who, when, where, what?
3. Complicating action: then what happened?
4. Evaluation: so what, how is this interesting?
5. Resolution: what finally happened?
6. Coda: bridging back to the following situation.

A typical narrative, according to Labov (1972), must have a set of sequentially related set of events reporting a change from one state to another and this reported change of state should be interesting, instructive, entertaining and worth telling. Though the structural properties isolated by Labov were developed with reference to oral narratives we can use them in our analysis of written narratives too. Pritchet's short story *The Fly in the Ointment* develops through descriptive passages, direct speech and free indirect speech. The interlocking of these various modes of narration has been dexterously done in the body of the text, and by using Labov's model we can isolate the following phases in its narrative structure:

1. Abstract: The title *The Fly in the Ointment* may be called the abstract of the story because it sketches the narrative in a nutshell. The title tells us that the story is about something that spoils a situation or an activity, and prevents something else from being as successful as it was expected to be.
2. Orientation: The section beginning with 'It was the dead hour' and ending with 'The son besides him was round-shouldered and shabby, a keen but anxious fellow in need of a hair-cut and going bald' is the orientation of the story, as it specifies the participants and circumstances of the narrative. This orientation may also be called the 'setting' of the story, because it is this section that creates the spatio-temporal setting of the narrative.

Orientation is very important in the narrative structure of a story; because while reading narratives, readers look for spatio-temporal indications of just what and how the incidents narrated happened. A study of the lexical items, deictic terms, and syntactical structures of *The Fly in the Ointment* points out how textual means are exploited by the narrator to articulate the 'orientation' or the setting of the story.

The orientation comes through in the first sixty-three lines. The story begins with a shifting perspective, it seems that the camera first captures a panoramic view, and then there is a close-up shot. The *ceiling of level mud coloured clouds, the mass of older buildings, the streets, the desert of public buildings*—these are shots from a distance. When the camera takes a close-up shot it records *latest office buildings, the road to the main station, an interval of two hundred or so, the next patch of shop fronts, a taxi outside one of the underground stations* and *a man of thirty-five* who made off down *one of the small streets*.

The definite article *the* is used in a semi-deictic capacity to introduce an element of familiarity and immediacy in the fictional world presented in the story. The sense of 'illusory subjectivity' is created by using *the* fourteen times in the span of the first ten lines: *the* dead hour, *the* ceiling, *the* latest office building, *the* city, *the* mass of older buildings, *the* street, *the* few cars, *the* few people, *the* roadway, *the* pavement, *the* road, *the* main station, *the* desert, *the* next patch of shop fronts

Pritchett is very particular in maintaining the sequence of his narrative details. The spatial background is very minutely described:

The city
The streets
One of the small streets
Among these streets

Similarly, the factory is described with photographic fidelity:

outside the factory
the machine room
the showroom
the glass door of the office

The orientation itself starts with a temporal reference: *it was the dead hour of a November afternoon*. Other temporal references are as follows:

his father's last day
the last day of thirty years' work
only a month's bankrupt

The orientation or setting also creates the necessary environment, which adds to the overall meaning of the narrative. It is noticed that in spite of the element of familiarity introduced in the opening paragraphs of the story, a sense of disorientation pervades these paragraphs. The latest office buildings stood out alarmingly like new tombstones, but the mass of older buildings is not compared to anything else. Did they look like old tombstones? There is also a note of devitalisation of humanity—people and cars are juxtaposed. The few *cars* and the *few people appeared and disappeared*, and *they* were not following the *roadway* or the *pavement*, but some *inner, personal route*. Both the cars and the people can appear and disappear, but the roadway is for the cars and the pavement for the people. Moreover, only the *people* can follow some *inner, personal route*. The juxtaposition of the cars and the people and the use of *they* for both cars and the people, give the impression of a blurred vision—it seems that in the city of the tombstones the opposition between animate and inanimate objects is neutralised.

Orientational features related to time create an unsettling effect. It is the dead hour of a November afternoon—on the one hand it specifies the month, the afternoon and the dead hour, but on the other hand it makes a vague reference to any day in the month of November. It is the young man's father's *last day* at his factory, it is his father's *last day* after thirty year's work; but the repetition of the last day does not help us to fix the temporal reference at a particular time. We are not told when the span of thirty years began.

Besides the presentation of a spatio-temporal setting and the creation of an environment, the orientation also gives the readers the reasons for the initial narrative incitement, and introduces the dramatis personae. The fourth and the fifth paragraphs tell us why the son is going to meet his father. He wants to help his father in his hour of financial crisis:

I must see him.

I must help him.

Both the sentences are in free direct speech, both of them use the same 'modal', and both the sentences are exactly equivalent from the structural point of view. The equivalence of the form of these two sentences suggests the importance of seeing and helping the father. These two sentences are foregrounded in the body of the text, and it is no wonder that the story is based on the son's seeing his father and offering to help him to ease his financial crisis. But, the fact that the son is going to see and help his father to tide over a financial crisis may not be a strong reason for the initial narrative incitement. Hence, the narrator inserts a clue in the following sentence:

All the same, knowing his father, he had paid off the taxi and walked the last quarter of a mile.

The father and the son are introduced as a part of the orientation. But it is significant to note that in comparison with the son, the father is more elaborately portrayed by the narrator

The father	*The son*
Old man	man of thirty-five
Vigorous, broad man	round shouldered
Clipped white hair	shabby
Well dressed	keen but anxious fellow
Snowman	
Pleased, blue eyes	
Pleased, impish smile	

3. *Complicating action:* The complicating action of the story comes mainly through the direct speech of the two protagonists in the section beginning with 'come in, Professor' and ending with 'I'd raise it somehow'. This section is temporally ordered and constitutes the longest section of the story. The father appears to be a man of split personality and 'the son noticed for the first time that like all big-faced men his father had two faces'. The fly episode reveals the father's determined effort to achieve his goal. He fails to drive away the fly and acknowledges his weakness for money. During the long verbal

exchange, the father plays a domineering role, and stops the son from speaking on two occasions:

a. The son began again, but *his father* stopped him

b. The son was about to speak. *The father* stopped.

From *his father* he has become *The father*. The two actions, the son beginning to speak and the father stopping him, occur in the same sentence a. joined by a punctuation mark. But in b. the two actions occur in two separate sentences.

The isolated sentences create a distancing effect; the son is no more controlled by the father. Until now, the father controlled the scene, but now the son is going to control the action, he is about to spell out the purpose of his visit. The narrative has reached the climax.

4. *Resolution and Coda:* The last section of the story beginning with 'He coloured...' and ending with 'Where, by when?' may be called both resolution and coda, because this section tells us what finally happened, provides a sense of completeness, and brings the narrator and the listener to the point at which they entered the story.

Except for the last three lines, this section is mainly descriptive. From 'He coloured' to 'on a writing pad' the actors recede in to the background and the narrator reports and evaluates the action of the protagonists.

With its well-defined structural properties, the text creates a sense of aesthetic balance, and highlights the message of the narrative. The old man was about to attain salvation, but he succumbed to his weakness for money and spoilt the chance of healing his wounded soul.

6.1.3 Grammaticisation of Plot Structure

Grammar and the plot structure are linked together in *The Fly in the Ointment*.The first paragraph of the story presents a dull and dreary picture of a November afternoon. The events described in this paragraph are either static or without any specific goal. Except for the verb *follow*, all other verbs are intransitive, and even the transitive verb follow is used in a negative construction—'they were not following'. Office buildings of the city stood out alarmingly, the few cars and the people *appeared* and *disappeared* slowly, one or two beggars were *dribbling* slowly. The repetition of the adverb *slowly* indicates the absence of speed. It is significant to note that the word *dribbling* itself implies a slow movement, but in order to emphasise the slow, eventless and dull life of a winter evening, the narrator says 'they were dribbling slowly'. In the background of this slow movement of men and things, the second paragraph takes off at a great speed. By putting *presently* in the thematic position of the first sentence of the second paragraph, the narrator makes a breakthrough, this proximal deictic term contrasts sharply with the monotonous, repetitive drudgery of the opening paragraph. The slow movement of men and cars must have been going on for a long time, but *presently* is oriented to the narrator/listener's narrative present. The phrasal verb *made off* has a teleological status of events in the narrative. The verb 'make off' means leaving a place as quickly as possible, often in order to escape, and hence, the statement 'a man of thirty-five paid his fare and made off down one of the small streets' is bound to arouse the listener / reader's curiosity and interest. The listener or the reader may wonder what could be the cause of such a rush.

The sentence 'He was going to see his father.' in the fourth paragraph, is related to the events *made off* and *was going* and hence, they add a dynamic force to the narrative. Moreover, just as the second paragraph introduces the son, the fourth paragraph introduces the father. (There is a reference to the father in the third paragraph, but here he is just an old man, and as the term is used in inner speech, it is not a part of the narrative technique).

The fifth paragraph explains why the young man is going to see his father. The last sentence of this paragraph 'All the same, knowing his father, he had paid off the taxi and walked the last quarter of a mile.' has a plot-structuring status. The verb *knows* is a stative verb describing an unconscious process of perception, but for the young man this *knowing* is a conscious process. In spite of his deep concern and sympathy for his father, he is well aware of his nature. Following Barthes' classificatory labels of a narrative, we may term this sentence as 'function' as it directs the narrative to its concluding point or message and achieves 'the overarching coherence of the narrative'

(Toolan, 1988). The young man knows his father, but the reader is kept in suspense until the last paragraph of the story. This sentence is connected with the single sentence of the second paragraph—'paid his fare and made off', and the first sentence of the fourth paragraph—'he was going to see his father'. The anaphoric references made by this sentence point out how all the sentences having a plot-structuring status make a narrative chain of texts.

In the sixth paragraph, the statement 'He pressed the bell' has a teleological status. In the background of the stative verbs *be, hear,* and *see* the dynamic verb *press* appears quite prominently, and pushes the narrative to the next stage.

When the son reaches the office and is received by his father, the dialogue carries on the narrative. The speed of the narrative gets momentum when the father draws his son's attention to the fly buzzing around. The fly episode uses some dynamic verbs to lead the action forward, and to indicate the old man's determined effort to achieve his goal. The old man *pulled* a duster out of a drawer and struck at the fly. He also *got on top* of his table and *snapped* the duster at the fly. When the old man failed to drive away the fly, he *got down* from the table very heavily, slowly and cautiously. The moment of his self-realisation is about to dawn on him, and the 'son felt as though a sun *had risen*'. The sentence 'Now, like the harvest moon in full glow, the father's face *shone up* at his son.' carries the narrative to the climax (italics added).

The moment the son spells out the specific purpose of his visit, the narrative moves forward very quickly. The paragraph that follows the son's offer of help records the son's embarrassment. Stative verbs of perception abound in this passage: *coloured, hated, knew, was ashamed, dreaded, understand*. In the background of these stative verbs dynamic verbs of the next paragraph have a high teleological status of events in the narrative, and all the four sentences of this paragraph have a high plot-structuring status:

> The father's *sailing* eyes *came down* and *looked* at his son's nervous, frowning face, and slowly the dreaming look *went* from the father's face. Slowly the harvest moon *came down*

> from its rosy voyage. The little face suddenly *became* dominant between the outer folds of skin like a fox *looking out* of a hole of clay. He *leaned* forward brusquely on the table and somehow a silver topped pencil was in hand *preparing* to note something briskly on a writing pad.
>
> (italics added)

The narrative events communicated by the dynamic verbs bring the story to its ultimate resolution—the father who had expressed a desire for renunciation of money has again been trapped in the web of money.

Besides the verbs, adverbs also add to the narrative speed of the plot. The little face suddenly became dominant. He leaned forward brusquely on the table and started preparing something briskly.

6.1.4 Grammaticisation of characters

While reading *The Fly in the Ointment*, we get the impression that characterisation is the narrator's forte, and the whole narrative centers on the portrait of the father. Using the model of grammaticisation of characters advocated by Toolan (1988), let us see how Pritchett used grammar to portray his protagonists.

The young man meets his father, listens to him patiently, and smiles occasionally to hide his irritation. Now, instead of the father doing things, his voice, his eyes, and face are given as performing their action:

> voice going dead
> nostrils fidgeting
> lips of this little face were speaking

It seems that the father is driven by a force which he is unable to bring under control. He is a man with a split personality. He is changed into his other self involuntarily, and the description of voice, nostrils, eyes and lips as doers indicates this transformation.

Pritchett often uses grammar as a visual metaphor. The description starts with the progressive form—going, fidgeting, but it is significant to note that the narrator uses aspect without tense, and this separation of aspect as a grammatical feature from the general category of tense, symbolises the separation of oneself from the other. After the recurrence of the progressive form, the description is in the simple past: 'his eyes *went* hard'. The use of *went* instead of showing going indicates that the process of transformation is complete.

When the father is about to regain his former self, his voice and nose are again given as performing their action:

> Ring in the hard voice began to soften.
> His thick nose sniffed.

The narrator now uses *began* instead of 'beginning', and *sniffed* instead of 'sniffing'. The order is now being restored.

When the father fails to drive away the fly and is exhausted, he again ceases to be a doer:

> his body began to sag
> a look of weakness came on to his face

When the son spells out the specific purpose of his visit, the father succumbs to the temptation, he is restless and his other self gets the upper hand. He is again driven by a force which he cannot control, and hence:

> sailing eyes came down
> the dreaming look went from the father's face
> the little face suddenly became dominant
> pencil... preparing to note something

The aggressive nature of the father and the defensive nature of the son are very vividly portrayed in the following physical movement of the two protagonists:

> The son leaned back instinctively
> The father... leaned forward
> As his son leaned back

The father's outward appearance is emphasised throughout the story. The use of modifiers in describing the father's eyes and face is quite significant. He has

> *pleased* blue eyes
> *pleased* impish smile
> *rosy* face
> *purplish* face

Modifiers like pleased or impish very aptly reveal the character of the father. The son's eyes or face is never described. He is just an anxious fellow eager to help his father out of a financial crisis. The opposing characters of the two protagonists are revealed even in the syntactical structures:

He struck again and the son struck too as the fly came down.

6.1.5 Thought and Speech Presentation in the Story

As already discussed in chapter 3, Leach and Short (1981) have classified 'speech and thought presentation in fiction into five categories:'

Narrative Report of Speech Act/ Thought Act NRSA/NRTA
Indirect Speech/Thought IS/IT
Free direct Speech/Thought FIS/FIT
Direct Speech/Thought DS/DT
Free Direct Speech/Thought FDS/FDT

The narrator's choice of a particular form of thought presentation is important, because when a narrator chooses to represent the thought of a character, the readers are invited to see things from that character's point of view.

As soon as the man of thirty-five made off down one of the small streets, the narrator describes the man's mental landscape. 'Better not arrive in a taxi, he was thinking'—it is an example of free indirect thought, which puts us directly inside the character's mind, because we get a vivid and immediate representation of the young man's thoughts. The next sentence 'the old man will wonder where I got the money' is in free direct thought. FDT is now used to show the more reflective side of the young man's nature. The shift from FIT to FDT has thus a stylistic effect. The FIT refers to the immediate reaction of the young man when he started walking; the FDT justifies his action when he was walking the small streets.

The FDT of 'I must see him. I must help him.' also reveals the reflective side of the young man. The readers are prompted to see things from the point of view of the son.

When the son meets his father, the dialogue goes on in DS. 'The whole train, the old man said, was practically packed with bankrupts every morning'—this is in IS. The narrator is now an interpreter between his readers or listeners and the words of his protagonist. Until now, he had been quoting the speech acts that occurred between the two protagonists. But now, he intervenes directly—this IS is foregrounded to emphasise the father's defensive strategy, and it prepares us for a further stylistic shift. FIS follows next: 'Thousands had gone. Thousands? Tens of Thousands. Some of the biggest men in the city were broke.' The use of FIS in this context has a distancing effect; the reader or listener is distanced from the character's words.

Direct speech
Indirect speech
Free indirect speech

When the father stops defending himself, the narrator describes the son's reaction. The narrator here uses free direct thought to speed up the effect of the thinking process, and to describe the agitated mind of the protagonist. Here, the narrator is not an intermediary, and the use of FDT reflects the abrupt change in the emotional contour of the son's character.

6.2. *THE BOARDING HOUSE*

James Joyce's short story *The Boarding House* describes 'an affair' between Polly, the daughter of Mrs Mooney who runs a boarding house and a young boarder. Mrs Mooney's boarding house is occupied by music-hall performers, tourists and a few young Dublin clerks. When Mrs Mooney's daughter, Polly becomes involved with one of the borders, Mr Doran, a clerk in his mid-thirties, Mrs Mooney doesn't interfere, she rather allows the affair to continue till the other boarders have noticed it. At an opportune moment she insists that Mr Doran marry her daughter. Mr Doran, who has already started to worry about his involvement with Polly, is worried that his employer might get to know of his affair with Polly. He also fears that Poly might try to 'put an end to herself' if he does not marry her. Knowing full, well that his family will look down on this marriage as Polly belongs to a lower social class, Mr Doran agrees to marry her.

While reading the story we get an intuitive feeling that the story is narrated from the perspectives of three characters: Mrs Mooney, Mr

Doran and Polly and a stylistic analysis of the story confirms this intuitive feeling.

6.2.1 Character Portrayal

The story begins with Mrs Mooney who makes a thematic presence in the first sentence of the story. A reading of the first two paragraphs of the story gives us an intuitive feeling that it is Mrs Mooney who will dominate the scene. Let us look at the following sentences:

a. *Mrs Mooney* was a butcher's daughter.

b. *She* was a woman who was quite able to keep things to herself: a determined woman.

c. *She* had married her father's foreman

d. *She* went to the priest and got a separation from him with care of the children.

e. *She* would give him neither money nor food nor house-room;

f. *Mrs Mooney*, who had taken what remained of her money out of the butcher business.

g. *She* governed the house cunningly and firmly.

While the story begins with sentences having Mrs Mooney or she in the thematic position it comes to an end with a number of sentences having Polly or she in the thematic position. Let us look at the following sentences:

a. *Polly* sat for a little time on the side of the bed, crying.

b. Then *she* dried her eyes and went over to the looking-glass.

c. *She* dipped the end of the towel in the water-jug and refreshed her eyes with the cool water.

d. *She* looked at herself in profile and readjusted a hairpin above her ear.

e. Then *she* went back to the bed again and sat at the foot.

f. *She* regarded the pillows for a long time and the sight of them awakened in her mind secret, amiable memories.

g. *She* rested the nape of her neck against the cool iron bed-rail and fell into a reverie.

h. *She* waited on patiently, almost cheerfully, without alarm, her memories gradually giving place to hopes and visions of the future.

i. At last *she* heard her mother calling.

j. *She* started to her feet and ran to the banisters.

k. Then *she* remembered what she had been waiting for.

Let us now look at the sentences which refer to Mr Doran:

a. She noticed that something was going on between Polly and one of the young men.

b. She would have lots of time to have the matter out with Mr Doran

c. She had allowed him to live beneath her roof, assuming that he was man of honour and he had simply abused her hospitality.

d. He was thirty-four or thirty-five years of age, so that youth could not be pleaded as his excuse; nor could ignorance be his excuse since he was a man who had seen something of the world.

e. He had simply taken advantage of Polly's youth.

f. The question was: what reparation would he make?

A study of the lexical items used to describe the three characters that help us to visualise them in a proper perspective.

Mrs Mooney	Polly	Mr Doran
a butcher's daughter a determined woman a big imposing woman the Madam an outraged mother Missus mamma	the madam's daughter a slim girl perverse Madona a young woman the girl his sister dear	one of the young men the young man a man of honour a serious young man the celibate the lover

Lexical items describing Mrs Mooney and Polly belong to one group while those describing Mr Doran belong to another. Mrs Mooney undergoes a transformation from a daughter to a wife and then to a mother. Polly is also presented as a daughter, a girl, a young woman and a sister. Both the mother and the daughter are presented in the background of their family, and like all other human beings they grow from one stage to another. But, Mr Doran is a static character; he does not undergo any transformation. His family background is also missing.

Mrs Mooney and her daughter are introduced directly. They occupy the thematic position in the sentences in which they are introduced for the first time.

> *Mrs Mooney* was a butcher's daughter.
> *Polly Mooney*, the Madam's daughter, would also sing.

Mr Doran's introduction is rather indirect. His name is not mentioned in the sentence which introduces him for the first time. He is just 'one of the young men' and he appears in the 'rheme' of the sentence. He is denied a thematic position.

Something was going on between Polly and *one of the young men.*

While describing Polly, Joyce is quite specific, but there is a lack of specificity in the description of Mr Doran. Polly was a slim girl of *nineteen* but Mr Doran was *thirty-four* or *thirty-five years* of age. Mr Doran was a man who had seen something of the world; Polly was set to do *house-work*. Mrs Mooney had allowed Mr Doran to live beneath her roof *assuming* that he was a man of honour.

6.2.2 Lexical Chain

A study of the lexical items helps us to get a glimpse of the opposing worlds of Mrs Mooney and Mr Doran.

Mrs Mooney	Mr Doran
a butcher's shop money house room tourists credit business broken bread a sum of money reparation marriage	Catholic wine merchant's shop Sunday morning confession the priest sin reparation God religious duties celibate

Mr Doran is a celibate, not an ordinary bachelor. He thinks of *reparation* in the background of his sin and confession. Mrs Mooney thinks of *reparation* in the background of *money* and *marriage*. The material world of Mrs Mooney and the spiritual world of Mr Doran stand opposed to each other and proceed towards the climax.

The story begins with a number of transitive verbs but the moment Mrs Mooney starts playing mind games, she falls back on verbs of perception.

Mrs Mooney	Mr Doran
intervened reconstruct suspect allowed thought counted felt was sure	knew felt his heart heard remembered echoed longed imagined

It seems that neither Mrs Mooney nor Mr Doran has any control over the events as they unfold. They just react to what happens. The story is essentially a war of nerves—it is fought on a psychological plane. Most of the verbs used with reference to Polly are verbs denoting physical action having specific goals. Polly represents the world of action, she sets the ball rolling, her mother and her lover have no other option but to react to what she does. Polly is the doer so far as the following verbs of action are concerned:

tapped	dried
entered	dipped
threw	refreshed
lit	readjusted
steadied	rested
started	ran

6.2.3 Grammar

The repeated use of the modal auxiliary *would* brings out the tension generated in the minds of the protagonists:

She *would* have lots of time
She was sure she *would* win
The affair *would* be sure to be talked
His employer *would* be certain
What reparation *would* he make
Some mothers *would* be content
She *would* not do so
The family *would* look down
What *would* grammar matter
She *would* put an end
He *would* never hear

6.2.4 Speech Presentation

Joyce uses Free Indirect Speech (FIS) and Free Indirect Thought (FIT) quite extensively in the story to bring a sense of authenticity and immediacy in the narrative. Instead of describing Mr Doran's disturbed state of mind with the help of IT, Joyce uses FIT:

> The harm was done. What could he do now but marry her or run away? He could not brazen it out. The affair would be sure to be talked of and his employer would be certain to hear of it. Dublin is such a small city: everyone knows everyone else's business.

When Polly came to Mr Doran in the morning and cried, her speech is presented in Free Direct Speech:

> "O Bob! Bob! What am I to do? What am I to do at all?"

But her words are presented in FIS when she serves the ultimatum:

> *She would put an end to herself, she said.*

Whose voice do we hear in these words? Polly's or the narrator's? Polly's voice mingles with that of the narrator. The narrator could say: She said that she would put an end to herself. But he preferred FIS to IS as a stylistic device.

A stylistic analysis of the story indicates that Mrs Mooney was determined to ensnare Mr Doran and, therefore, she bade her time before intervening at the opportune moment. While describing the happenings of a Sunday morning the narrator uses different points of view. Though the narration starts from Mrs Mooney's point of view it soon shifts to Mr Doran's point of view.

6.2.5 Summing up

The stylistic analysis of the two short stories, *The Fly in the Ointment* and *The Boarding House* indicates the eclectic approach of stylistics. There are no hard and fast rules that all the tools of stylistics must be used rigorously in the stylistic analysis of all literary texts. As the ultimate objective of stylistics is to validate our intuitive responses to a text, the stylistician is at liberty to choose the stylistic tools necessary for the stylistic analysis of a particular text.

Exercises

1. Write a note on Labov's six-part structure of a fully-formed oral narrative and analyse a short story following Labov's model.
2. Take a short story by any author of your choice and analyse it following the model of grammaticisation of plot structure and character presented in the study of *The Fly in the Ointment*.
3. Analyse the 'thought and speech presentation' in James Joyce's short story, *Eveline*.

7

Analysing Drama Texts

7.1 STYLISTIC ANALYSIS OF DISCOURSE

Short (1989) points out how a discourse stylistic analysis of drama texts can bring out the inner meaning conveyed by a playwright. He says that drama texts should be treated as a set of communicative acts and not just as a configuration of phonetic, syntactic and lexical patterns. He also observes that the following major categories may be fruitfully used in the analysis of a drama text:

a. Speech Acts
b. Presuppositions
c. The co-operative principle in conversation
d. Terms of address

7.1.1 Speech Acts

The theory of speech acts as propounded by Austin (1962) maintains that producing an utterance actually means doing things. When a speaker says 'I will do it tomorrow,' he not only makes a statement, he also promises to do it tomorrow. Making a promise is a speech act performed by a speaker with respect to his addressee. Short says that a speech act is 'dramatically' important at the beginning of plays and when new characters are introduced (Short, 1996). Consider the beginning of Ibsen's *A Doll's House*:

Nora: Hide the Christmas tree carefully, Helen. Make sure the children don't see it till this evening, when it is decorated. (*To the Porter, taking out her purse*) How much?

Porter: Six pence.

Nora: There is a shilling. No, keep the change.

(*A Doll's House*, Act I)

Nora's speech act which can be characterised as a *directive*, enables her to command or direct the maid to do something, that is, to hide the Christmas tree carefully till the evening. It also tells us of her superior position. The utterance 'How much?' is also a directive in the sense that this speech act directs the porter to tell her how much he wants from her. When she says, 'There is a shilling.' she is actually performing the act of giving a shilling to the porter. A speech act that commits a speaker to doing some thing is termed as a verdictive by Austin and, therefore, the utterance 'There is a shilling.' is a verdictive speech act. 'No, keep the change.' is a speech act that brings out the state of affairs; she does not want the porter to return her the balance amount. It is a declaration on her part.

Now, consider the opening of Oscar Wilde's *The Importance of Being Earnest:*

Algernon: Did you hear what I was playing, Lane?

Lane: I didn't think it polite to listen, Sir.

Algernon: I'm sorry for that, for your sake. I don't play accurately—any one can play accurately—but I play with wonderful expression. As far as the piano is concerned, sentiment is my forte. I keep science for life

Lane: Yes, Sir.

Algernon: And, speaking of the science of life, have you got the cucumber sandwiches cut for Lady Bracknell?

(*The Importance of Being Earnest*, Act I)

We notice that as soon as Algernon appears on the stage he performs the act of questioning Lane, the servant. As a speech act it belongs to the category of directives. Lane, on the other hand, makes a representative speech act as his speech merely represents a state of affair, he makes a statement. The second speech by Algernon is an expressive speech act as it expresses his psychological attitude towards an event. The answer 'Yes, Sir.' is again a representative speech act.

The next speech by Algernon is a directive speech act as he is questioning his servant. That Algernon is the master and Lane is the servant is evident from the nature of the speech act performed by them. The master performs directive or expressive speech acts, whereas the servant can only perform representative speech acts.

7.1.2 Presuppositions

When a speaker initiates a conversation, he makes assumptions about what kind of knowledge that is already available to his addressee and his speech is made in the context of the knowledge already known to the addressee. These assumptions made by the addressee are termed as presupposition by discourse analysts. What a speaker utters and what he presupposes are equally important for decoding the message of a text. Consider the following extract from *Hamlet*:

Marcellus: Holla, Barnardo!

Barnardo: Say. What is Horatio there?

Horatio: A piece of him.

Barnardo: Welcome, Horatio. Welcome, good Marcellus.

Horatio: What, has this thing appear'd again to night?

Barnardo: I have seen nothing.

(*Hamlet*, Act I, Scene I)

While Horatio asked Barnardo if he had seen the apparition on that particular night he presupposed that Barnardo had seen the apparition on a previous occasion. In the following dialogue Algernon presupposed that Lane had listened to him when he was playing the piano:

Algernon: Did you hear what I was playing, Lane?

Lane: I didn't think it polite to listen, Sir.

(*The Importance of Being Earnest*, Act I)

7.1.3 The Co-operative Principle in Conversation

The co-operative principle in conversation, according Grice (1975), tries to capture the implicature of a statement made by an addresser to his addressee. Grice asserts that an addressee can decode the meaning of a message only when he can make a distinction between 'sentence meanings' and 'utterance meaning'. A sentence may have a general meaning, but when a speaker in a particular context uses it, it may convey a different meaning. Grice says that the addressee can infer the meaning conveyed by a message framed by the addresser when both of them share the Co-operative Principle of Conversation, which is based on four conversational maxims:

a. the maxim of quantity	Say what is appropriate—not too much or too little .
b. the maxim of quality	Be truthful.
c. the maxim of manner	Avoid ambiguity and give information in an appropriate order.
d. the maxim of relevance	Be relevant, avoid unnecessary prolixity.

These maxims, Grice admits, are often not adhered to by the speakers with the tacit approval of both the addresser as well as the addressee.

A: How much did you get in your major paper?
B: Poor marks.

B's answer does not adhere to the maxim of quantity as he does not provide the appropriate answer. The maxim of quality is not adhered to by a speaker when he makes a statement that he knows to be untrue. The maxim of manner is not followed by a speaker when he uses ambiguity in his speech and does not supply the information in an appropriate order.

A: Are you waiting for a city bus?
B: All sorts of transport are available here.

B does not respond to A's question as per the maxim of manner. He says all sorts of transport are available, and, therefore, he may be waiting for a bus or for a taxi.

The maxim of relevance is not adhered to by a speaker when he does not provide a relevant answer.

A: When will the holidays begin this year?
B: I am preparing for my exams

B's answer is not at all related to A's question and, therefore, it flouts the maxim of relevance.

7.1.4. Politeness

Brown and Levinson (1987) suggest that politeness is a universal phenomenon, affecting linguistic and other social behaviour. In any social interaction the members of any social group try to be polite in their use of language. Suppose, you are angry with your friend for something that he has done. You can tell him, 'You should not have done that.' But instead of telling him bluntly that he has done something bad you could say, 'If I were you I would not have done that.' In any polite conversation, a speaker phrases directives as requests, not commands, and makes them very indirect. Consider the following utterances:

1. Pass on the salt please.
2. Will you pass on the salt please?
3. Could I ask you to pass on the salt please?
4. Would you mind passing me the salt?

The last two utterances mentioned above are more polite than the first two utterances. The indirect request often gives the addressee a linguistic option of merely answering a question without complying with the request.

Short (1996) remarks that though politeness in speech is the accepted norm of social interaction, a lot of impoliteness is noticed in the speeches of the dramatis personae. He argues that impoliteness in the dialogues of a drama is a way of indicating social conflict.

7.1.5 Terms of address

A study of the terms of address used by the characters reveals the social positions and the role-relations of the dramatis personae. The variation of attitudes towards one another is reflected in the terms of address used by the characters in a conversation. As Short points out, 'Title plus last name and *Sir* plus first name can be used by people of inferior status when addressing social superiors. Last name alone is used by close equals or by people of superior status to well-known inferiors.' Consider how Kent addresses the king in the following extract taken from Shakespeare's *King Lear*:

Lear: To thee and thine hereditary ever
Remain this ample third of our fair kingdom,
No less in space, validity and pleasure
Than that conferred on Goneril.– But now our joy,
Although our last and least, to whose young love
The vines of France and milk of Burgundy
Strive to be interessed, what can you say to draw
A third more opulent than your sisters? Speak.
Cordelia: Nothing, my lord.
Lear: Nothing?
Cordelia: Nothing.
Lear: How, nothing will come of nothing. Speak again.
Cordelia: Unhappy that I am, I cannot heave
My heart into my mouth, I love your majesty
According to my bond, no more nor less.
Lear: How, how, Cordelia? Mend your speech a little,
Lest you may mar your fortunes.
Cordelia: Good my lord,
You have begot me, bred me, loved me. I
Return those duties back as are right fit,
Obey you, love you and most honour you.
Why have my sisters husbands, if they say
They love you all? Haply when I shall wed,
That lord whose hand must take my plight shall carry
Half my love with him, half my care and duty.
Sure I shall never marry like my sisters
To love my father all.
Lear: But goes thy heart with this?
Cordelia: Ay, my good lord.
Lear: So youthful and so untender?
Cordelia: So young, my lord and true.
Lear: Well, let it be so. Thy truth then be thy dower,
For by the sacred radiance of the sun,
The mysteries of Hecate and the night,
By all the operation of the orbs

From whom we do exist and cease to be,
Here I disclaim my paternal care
Propinquity and property of blood,
And as a stranger to my heart and me
Hold thee from this for ever. The barbarous Scythian,
Or he that makes his generation messes
To gorge his appetite, shall to my bosom
Be as well neighboured, pitied and relieved,
As thou my sometime daughter.

Kent: Good my liege—

Lear: Peace, Kent,
Come not between the dragon and his wrath!
I loved her most, and thought to set my rest
On her kind nursery. [*to Cordelia*] Hence and avoid my sight.
So be my grave my peace, as here I give
Her father's heart from her. Call France. Who stirs?
Call Burgundy.

(*Attendants rush off*)

Cornwall and Albany,
With my two daughters' dowers, digest this third.
Let pride, which she calls plainness, marry her.
I do invest you jointly with my power,
Pre-eminence and all the large effects
That troop with majesty. Ourself by monthly course,
With reservation of an hundred knights
By you to be sustained, shall our abode
Make with you by due turn; only we shall retain
The name, and all th'addition to a kind: the sway,
Revenue, execution of the rest,
Beloved sons, be yours; which to confirm,
This coronet part between you.

Kent: Royal Lear,
Whom I have ever honoured as my king,
Loved as my father, as my master followed,
As my great patron thought on in my prayers –

Lear: The bow is bent and drawn; make from the shaft.

Kent: Let it fall rather, though the fork invade
The region of my heart: be Kent unmannerly
When Lear is mad. What wouldst thou do, old man?
Think'st thou that duty shall have dread to speak,
When power to flattery bows? To plainness honour's bound
When majesty falls to folly, Reserve the state,
And in the best consideration check
This hideous rashness. Answer my life my judgement,
Thy youngest daughter does not love thee least,
Nor are those empty - hearted, whose low sounds
Reverb no hollowness.
Lear: Kent, on thy life, no more.
Kent: My life I never held but as a pawn
To wage against thine enemies, ne'er fear to lose it,
Thy safety being the motive.
Lear: Out of my sight!
Kent: See better, Lear, and let me still remain.

(*King Lear*, Act I, Scene I)

At first Kent addresses the King as *my liege* (a highly fomal term of address indicating humble submission), then he addresses the king as *Royal Lear* (the first name is used but with the honorific Royal), but when the king threatens to kill him, Kent addresses him by his first name, *Royal Lear* has become *Lear*, bereft of his royal grandeur. He even calls him an *old man*.

In order to understand the plot of a drama in its true perspective and to study the playwright's dramatic skill in the presentation of his characters, a stylistic analysis of the language used by the dramatis personae is of paramount importance. A playwright uses language as a resource to portray his characters and, therefore, a drama critic has to analyse the verbal interaction between characters as a tool for unfolding the dramatic skill of a playwright.

7.2. QUANTITY AND LENGTH OF THE SPEECH

The quantity and the length of the speech made by a character is indicative of the relative importance of the characters presented in a play. Major characters have generally longer and more speeches than the minor characters. Consider the following extract from Marlowe's *The Jew of Malta*:

Ferneze: Yes; give me leave. And, Hebrews, now come near.
From the Emperor of Turkey is arriv'd
Great Selim Calymath, his highness' son,
To levy of us ten years' tribute past:
Now, then, here know that is concerneth us.
Barabas: Then, good my lord, to keep your quiet still,
Your lordship shall do well to let them have it.
Ferneze: Soft, Barabas! There's more' longs to't than so.
To what this ten years' tribute will amount,
That we have cast, but cannot compass it
By reason of the wars, that robb'd our store;
And therefore are we to request your aid.
Barabas: Alas, my lord, we are no soldiers!
And what's our aid against so great a prince?
First Knight: Tut, Jew, we know thou art no soldier:
Thou art a merchant and money'd man,
And' tis thy money, Barabas, we seek.
Barabas: How, my lord! My money!
Ferneze: Thine and the rest.
For, to be short, amongst you't must be had.
First Jew: Alas, my lord, the most of us are poor!
Ferneze: Then let the rich increase your portions.
Barabas: Are strangers with your tribute to be tax'd?
Second Knight: Have strangers leave with us to get their wealth?
Then let them with us contribute.
Barabas: How? Equally?
Ferneze: No, Jew, like infidels;
For through our sufferance of your hateful lives,
Who stand accursed in the sight of heaven,
These taxes and afflictions are befall'n
And therefore thus we are determined.

(*The Jew of Malta*, Act I, Scene I)

As Ferneze, the Governor of Malta has a superior position to that of Barabas, the Jew and other minor characters, he has longer speeches than the other characters.

The length of the speech is also indicative of the power relation between characters. In the following extract quoted from *Macbeth*, the length of the speeches made by Macbeth and Lady Macbeth indicates the effacement of Macbeth in the presence of Lady Macbeth. In the beginning of the episode it is Macbeth who makes longer speeches but as he starts losing control over the situation and succumbs to his sense of guilt, his speeches become shorter and those of Lady Macbeth become longer.

Macbeth enters carrying two bloodstained daggers and tells his wife:

Macbeth: I have done the deed—Didst thou not hear a noise?
Lady Macbeth: I heard the owl scream, and the crickets cry.
Did not you speak?
Macbeth: When?
Lady Macbeth: Now
Macbeth: As I descended?
Lady Macbeth: Ay.
Macbeth: Hark!
Who lies I'th' second chamber?
Lady Macbeth: Donalbain
Macbeth: This is a sorry sight.
Lady Macbeth: A foolish thought to say a sorry sight.
Macbeth: There's one did laugh in's sleep and one cried,
"Murder!"
That they did wake each other: I stood and heard them;
But they did say their prayers, and address'd them
Again to sleep.
Lady Macbeth: There are two lodg'd together.
Macbeth: One Cried, "God bless us !" and , "Amen," the other,
As they had seen me with these hangman's hands.
List'ning their fear, I could not say, "Amen"
When they did say "God bless us"
Lady Macbeth: Consider it not so deeply.

Macbeth: But wherefore could not I pronounce "Amen"?
I had most need of blessing, and "Amen"
Stuck in my throat.
Lady Macbeth: These deeds must not be thought
After these ways: so, it will make us mad.
Lady Macbeth: Methought, I heard a voice cry, "Sleep no more!
Macbeth does murder Sleep," —the innocent Sleep;
Sleep that knits up the ravell'd sleave of care,
The death of each day's life, sore labour's bath,
Balm of hurt minds, great Nature's second course,
Chief nourisher in life's feast;—
Lady Macbeth: What do you mean?
Macbeth: Still it cried, "Sleep no more!" to all the house:
"Glamis hath murder'd Sleep, and therefore Cawdor
Shall sleep no more, Macbeth shall sleep no more!"
Lady Macbeth: Who was it that thus cried? Why, worthy Thane,
You do unbend your noble strength, to think
So brainsickly of things. Go, get some water,
And wash this filthy witness from your hand.—
Why did you bring these daggers from the place?
They must lie there: go, carry them, and smear
The sleepy grooms with blood.
Lady Macbeth: I'll go no more:
I am afraid to think what I have done;
Look on't again I dare not.
Lady Macbeth: Infirm of purpose!
Give me the dagger. The sleeping, and the dead,
Are but as pictures; 'tis the eye of childhood
That fears a painted devil. If he do bleed,
I'll gild the faces of the grooms withal,
For it must seem their guilt. [*Exit—Knocking within.*].
Macbeth: Whence is that knocking?—
How is't with me, when every noise appals me?
What hands are here? Ha! they pluck out mine eyes.
Will all great Neptune's ocean wash this blood
Clean from my hand? No, this my hand will rather

The multitudinous seas incarnadine,
Making the green one red.

Re-enter Lady Macbeth

Lady Macbeth: My hands are of your colour; but I shame
To wear a heart so white. [*Knock*] I hear a knocking
At the south entry:- retire we to our chamber.
A little water clears us of this deed: How easy is it then!
Your constancy
Hath left you unattended—[*Knock*] Hark ! more Knocking.
Get on you night- gown, lest occasion call us,
And show us to be watchers.—Be not lost
So poorly in your thoughts.

Macbeth: To know my deed, 'twere best not know myself. [*Knock.*
Wake Duncan with thy knocking: I would thou Couldst!
[*Exeunt.*

(*Macbeth*, Act II, Scene I)

The length of Lady Macbeth's speeches is in keeping with the dominating role she plays in this scene.

7.3 EXCHANGE SEQUENCES

Sinclair and Coulthard (1975) have identified a three-part exchange structure in their analysis of discourses—Initiation (I) Response (R) and Feedback (F). Consider the opening lines of Oscar Wilde's *The Importance of Being Earnest:*

Algernon: Did you hear what I was playing, Lane? (I)

Lane: I didn't think it polite to listen, Sir. (R)

Algernon: I'm sorry for that, for your sake. I don't play accurately— any one can play accurately—but I play with wonderful expression. As far as the piano is concerned, sentiment is my forte. I keep science for life (F)

(*The Importance of Being Earnest*, Act I)

Algernon initiates the discussion by asking a question, Lane responds with a negative note and consequently Algernon gives a detailed feedback on Lane's response. Though the real life conversation does not always follow the I-R-F model discussed above, playwrights often use this model with modifications wherever necessary.

Nash(1989) points out that the first task of the discourse analyst is to determine the structure of conversation as a complex of exchanges minimally represented as Initiation and Response. According to Nash 'Initiation' and 'Response' come under a broad category called 'interaction', which comprises transactions between certain speakers on certain topics and these transactions are realised as exchanges in a dramatic text. He further says that these exchanges are presented as various types of *moves* such as opening moves, supporting moves, challenging moves. All these moves are represented as verbal acts performed by the dramatis personae.

7.4 SUMMING UP

As drama is based on verbal interaction, a stylistic analysis of drama should try to find out how the relationships between people are constructed and negotiated in a dramatic text. A study of speech acts, presuppositions, the co-operative principle of conversation, the term of address and the exchange sequence can give us valuable clues to the understanding of the meaning of a drama text.

Exercises

1. Discuss Austin's *Theory of Speech Acts* with suitable examples drawn from any play read you have read.
2. What are the main arguments put forward by Grice in his co-operative principles in conversation?
3. Read the following extract from *Romeo and Juliet* and analyse it on the basis the use of terms of address, exchange sequence and the cooperative theory of conversation.

(Lord Capulet and Lady Capulet arrange their daughter, Juliet's marriage with Paris. But Juliet is already in love with Romeo, and she tells her mother that she is not ready to accept the marriage arranged by her parents. Lady Capulet now passes on the news to Lord Capulet)

Capulet: How now, wife!

Have you delivered to her our decree?

Lady Capulet: Ay, sir, but she will none, she gives you thanks.
I would the fool were married to her grave.

Capulet: Soft! Take me with you, take me with you, wife.
How will she none? Doth she not give us thanks?
Is she not proud? Doth she not count her blest?
Unworthy as she is, that we have wrought
So worthy a gentleman to be her bridegroom?

Juliet: Not proud you have, but thankful that you have.
Proud can I never be of what I hate.
But thankful even for hate that is meant love.

Capulet: How, how, how, how, chopp'd logic! What is this?
'Proud'—and 'I thank you'— and 'I thank you not'—
And yet not proud? Mistress minion, you,
Thank me no thankings, nor proud me no prouds,
But fettle your fine joints 'gainst Thursday next,
To go with Paris to Saint Peter's Church,
Or I will drag you on a hurdle thither.
Out, you green-sickness carrion! Out you baggage!
You tallow-face!

(*Romeo and Juliet*, Act III, Scene v)

8

English in Indian Newspapers A Stylistic Analysis

8.1 THE LANGUAGE OF NEWSPAPERS

Though style is a way in which language is used in a particular genre, stylistics has typically been concerned over the years only with literary language. As newspapers use language that is non-literary, analysis of newspaper texts have rarely been taken seriously.

Newspapers present a wide range of linguistically distinctive varieties of language. The assumption that the language of newspapers has a referential function only is rather too simplistic. Besides serving a referential function, the language of newspapers can also serve a persuasive or an emotive function in a very subtle way. In order to make their reporting convincing, appealing and eye-catching all the six functions of language—referential, emotive, connotive, phatic, metalinguistic, as postulated by Jakobson (1961) are skillfully exploited by newspapers. Though Halliday (1967) propounded the functions of language—ideational, interpersonal and textual— with reference to the literary language only, his findings can also be used with reference to the language of newspapers as well.

Newspapers are supposed to present information compactly, clearly, authoritatively and without any ambiguity. But newspaper reports throughout the world are usually coloured by opinion and Indian newspapers are no exception. A stylistic analysis of the language of Indian English newspapers reveals that though the ideational function of language is used to produce an apparently neutral view of reality, the interpersonal function of the language dominates the pages of these newspapers.

8.1.1. Indian English Newspapers

The language of the *Times of India*, the *Statesman*, the *Hindu*, The *Indian Express*, the *Asian Age* and the *Sentinel* is analysed in the following sections to find out the unique stylistic features of English used in these newspapers. The language of Indian English newspapers is a vibrant variety with a distinctive colour of its own. This variety conveys the message to the readers by using an accepted code of the language; it fits appropriately into a speech situation, fulfilling the required social designs that newspapers have on the readers, and it is also well constructed as a text. The functional significance of the language of these newspapers depends on the stylistic significance of the language.

Indian English newspapers use linguistic choices at the deep structure in order to effect their communicative functions at the surface structure. These papers are conditioned by the Indian socio-linguistic context. English newspapers in India cater to the needs of Indian bilinguals who use English as a second language in Indian social, educational and administrative contexts and, therefore, the following headlines which may not be acceptable to native speakers of English are quite intelligible to the Indian readers:

Team formed to curb fraud NGOs (the *Indian Express*, 23 October, 2002)

PM attacked with viral (the *Times of India*, 23 October, 2002)

Denied entry at garba, minister's son beats up 4 (the *Indian Express*, 18 October, 2002)

Advani brokers Parivar peace (the *Times of India*, 21 October, 2002)

High noise crackers banned (the *Hindu*, 18 October, 2002)

BJP gets backhand rebel slap (the *Asian Age*, 24 October, 2002)

The following headlines taken from the *Times of India* the *Hindu* and the *Indian Express* refer to the same incident and they may be taken as examples of the referential function of language.

West Indies fights back	(the *Hindu*, 19 October, 2002)
India runs into speed breakers	(the *Times of India*, 19 October, 2002)
Wicked wicket kills test cricket	(the *Indian Express*, 19 October, 2002)

But do these headlines merely state the facts? The headline of the *Hindu* has a neutral tone, but the two other headlines are presented from the point of view of the Indian readers. Would the newspapers published by a supporter of the West Indian team have appreciated such a headline? The language of newspapers not only communicates, it also propagates the ideology and the opinion of the newspaper. The intermingling of facts and opinions is a distinguishing stylistic feature of Indian English newspapers. Let us consider the following headlines referring to Uma Bharati's news conference:

Uma Bharati takes pot shots at Shourie (the *Hindu*, 23 October, 2002)

Uma Bharati to take Nelco debate to PM (the *Times of India*, 23 October, 2002)

Uma to take Nelco issue to PM (the *Indian Express*, 23 October, 2002)

For the *Hindu* and the *Times of India*, the Union Minister for Coal and Mines is Uma Bharati but for the *Indian Express* she is just Uma. By referring to Uma Bharti as Uma the *Indian Express* has followed the style of tabloid newspapers, not that of broadsheet newspapers. While the *Times of India* uses the formal word 'debate' (formal argument or discussion of a question), the *Indian Express* takes recourse to the commonly used word 'issue' (important topic for discussion). The *Hindu* is not interested in the factual information; it is interested in the interpretative function of the language. That the minister made a random attempt at Shourie without taking a careful aim is conveyed in the headline 'Uma Bharti takes pot shots at Shourie.'

The following texts are quite representative of the style of English writing noticed in Indian newspapers. All the four texts refer to the test match between India and West Indies played in Chennai on 17 October, 2002.

1. Even as the floodlights brightened up the arena when things were getting dark with clouds hovering around, the beleaguered West Indians, at last, spotted a sliver of light and hope, when there was nothing but darkness all around (the *Hindu*, 19 October 2002).
2. Under some enterprising leadership of Carl Hooper, the Caribbean staged a comeback of sorts on the second day of the second test on Friday when they reduced the powerful home team to 190 for

5 at draw of stumps with VVS Laxman, the last of the three recognised batsmen still to be dislodged (the *Times of India*, 19 October 2002).

3. This newly - laid MA Chidambaram Stadium strip is a disgrace of a Test pitch. And the proof of it was bountiful even though Friday was only the second day of the Test (the *Indian Express*, 19 October, 2002).
4. India took a 23-run first innings lead but not before they were made to toil by the West Indian bowlers who brought their side back into the match by dismissing the cream of the Indian batting on the second day of the second cricket test here today. (the *Sentinel*, 19 October 2002).

Should we call the style of the first text literary or journalistic? Is the language merely ideational? Is the *Hindu* communicating a message or is it narrating an incident from the point of view of the West Indies who were enveloped by the dark clouds? The floodlights, the clouds hovering around, a sliver of light and hope and the all pervasive darkness make this piece of news paper reporting a piece akin to a literary text.

Unlike the *Hindu*, the reporting of the *Times of India* is more factual than rhetorical. The *Indian Express* uses the report to vent its feeling and calls the stadium strip a disgrace of a test pitch. While the other papers reported the performance of the players, the *Indian Express* highlighted the poor quality of the stadium. The news of this paper is interpretative as well as subjective.

All the four reports can be studied from the point of view of discourse analysis. The theme (Halliday, 1967) is a formal category that serves as the point of any discourse. The themes or the starting points of the discourses of the above-mentioned reports on the test match are:

Even as the floodlights brighten up

Under some enterprising leadership

This newly laid MA Chidambaram Stadium strip

India took a 24 run-first inning lead

The discoursal process of thematisation plays an important role in the presentation of the text in newspapers. What the paper puts first influences the interpretation of everything that follows. The heading of the report influences the interpretation of the news items, the constituent which is thematised in a sentence of a report influences the interpretation of a sentence and the first sentence of the first paragraph of the whole report. A study of the themes and the rhymes (Brown and Yule,1983) of newspaper headlines shows the subtle way in which newspapers go beyond the ideational function of the language. The position of the 'themes' of the following headlines conditions the interpretation of the news items presented by the newspapers:

Kashmir demolishes dynasty *(*the *Times of India,* 11 October, 2002)

Uneasy calm in Jhajjar *(*the *Hindu*, 18 October, 2002)

5 Dalits lynched in Haryana (the *Indian Express*, 18 October, 2002)

Alert sounded in Jhajjar (the *Times of India*, 18 October, 2002)

Army grappling with logistics of pull back (the *Hindu*, 18 October, 2002)

Logistics makes pull back later than sooner (the *Indian Express,* 18 October, 2002)

In the sentence 'Army grappling with logistics of pull back', *Army* is the theme while in the sentence 'Logistics makes pull back later than sooner' *Logistics* is the theme. The choice of themes in these two reports indicates a conscious use of language by the two newspapers. the *Hindu* makes *Uneasy* the theme in its report 'Uneasy calm in Jhajjar' but the *Indian Express* makes *5 Dalits* the theme in its report '5 Dalits lynched in Haryana'. The use of themes in these reports serves the communicative needs of newspapers from their respective points of view. In the background of the themes used by these two newspapers the theme *Alert* used by the *Times of India* is just ideational. It adds to the neutral tone of the newspaper.

8.1.2 Summing up

A stylistic analysis of the language of newspapers reveals that a newspaper's vocabulary and the syntactic structure used, reflect the attitudes and the perception of the editorial staff to the incidents or events reported in the newspaper. Indian newspapers not only report events, they also interpret and explain the events by manipulating stylistics features.

Exercises

1. 'The language of newspapers not only communicates, it also propagates the ideology and the opinion of the newspaper'—Discuss with the help of some newspaper headlines selected by you from Indian English newspapers.
2. Read the following headlines used in Indian Newspapers and comment on their stylistic features:
   a. Rupee rise gives firms the jitters
   b. Manipur's agony moves drug firms
   c. India falter in run race
   d. Capital to Capitol Hill, Dismay and Despair
   e. War on the way we live
   f. India tops terror toll, after Iraq
   g. It's terror, no use denying it

Appendix–1

From *Mother and Daughter*

Virginia Bodoin had a good job; she was head of a department in a certain government office, held a responsible position, and earned, to imitate Balzac and be precise about it, seven hundred and fifty pounds a year. That is already something, Rachael Bodoin, her mother, had an income of about six hundred a year, on which she had lived in the capitals of Europe since the effacement of a never very important husband.

Now after some years of virtual separation and 'freedom', mother and daughter once more thought of settling down. They had become, in course of time, more like a married couple than mother and daughter. They knew one another very well indeed, and each was a little 'nervous' of the other. They had lived together and parted several times. Virginia was now thirty, and she didn't look like marrying. For four years she had been as good as married to Henry Lubbock, a rather spoilt young man who was musical. Then Henry let her down: for two reasons. He couldn't stand her mother. Her mother couldn't stand him. And anybody whom Mrs Bodoin could not stand she managed to sit on, disastrously. So Henry had writhed horribly, feeling his helpless mother-in-law sitting on him tight, and Virginia after all, in a helpless sort of family loyalty, sitting alongside her mother. Virginia didn't really want to sit on Henry. But when her mother egged her on, she couldn't help it. For ultimately her mother had power over her; a strange *female* power, nothing to do with parental authority. Virginia had long thrown parental authority to the winds. But her mother had another, much subtler form of domination, female and thrilling, so that when Rachael said: 'let's squash him!' Virginia had to rush wickedly and gleefully to the sport. And Henry knew quite well when he was being squashed. So that was one of his reasons for going back on Vinny. He called her Vinny, to the superlative disgust of Mrs Bodoin, who always corrected him: My daughter *Virginia*—.

The second reason was, again to be Balzacian, that Virginia hadn't a sou of her own. Henry had a sorry two hundred and fifty. But she was earning them. Whereas Henry managed to earn about twelve pounds per annum, by his precious music. He had realised that he would find it hard to earn more. So that marrying, except with a wife who could keep him, was rather out of the question. Vinny would inherit her mother's money. But then Mrs Bodoin had the health and muscular equipment of the Sphinx. She would live for ever, seeking whom she might devour, and devouring him. Henry lived with Vinny for two years, in the married sense of the words: and Vinny felt they were married, minus a mere ceremony. But Vinny had her mother always in the background, often as far back as Paris or Biarritz, but still, within letter reach. And she never realised the funny little grin that came on her own elvish face when her mother, even in a letter, spread her skirts and calmly sat on Henry. She never realised that in spirit she promptly and mischievously sat on him too; she could no more have helped it than the tide can help turning to the moon. And she did not dream that he felt it, and was utterly mortified in his masculine vanity. Women, very often, hypnotise one another, and then, hypnotised, they proceed gently to wring the neck of the man they think they are loving with all their hearts. Then they call it utter perversity on his part, that he doesn't like having his neck wrung. They think he is repudiating a heart-felt love. For they are hypnotised. Women hypnotise one another, without knowing it.

In the end, Henry backed out. He saw himself being simply reduced to nothingness by two women, an old witch with muscles like the Sphinx, and a young, spell-bound witch, lavish, elvish, and weak, who utterly spoilt him but who ate his marrow.

—*D.H. Lawrence*

Appendix–2

The Fly in the Ointment

It was the dead hour of a November afternoon. Under the ceiling of level mud-coloured cloud, the latest office buildings of the city stood out alarmingly like new tombstones, among the mass of older buildings. And along the streets, the few cars and the few people appeared and disappeared slowly as if they were not following the roadway or the pavement, but some inner, personal route. Along the road to the main station, at intervals of two hundred yards or so, unemployed men and one or two beggars were dribbling slowly past the desert of public buildings to the next patch of shop fronts.

Presently a taxi stopped outside one of the underground stations and a man of thirty-five paid his fare and made off down one of the small streets.

'Better not arrive in a taxi,' he was thinking. 'The old man will wonder where I got the money.'

He was going to see his father. It was his father's last day at his factory, the last day of thirty years' work and life among these streets, building a business out of nothing, and then, after a few years of prosperity, letting it go to pieces in a chaffer of rumour, idleness, quarrels, accusations, and at last, bankruptcy.

Suddenly all the money quarrels of the family, which nagged in the young man's mind, had been dissolved. His dread of being involved in them vanished. He was overcome by the sadness of his father's situation. 'Thirty years of your life come to an end. I must see him. I must help him.' All the same, knowing his father, he had paid off the taxi and walked the last quarter of a mile.

It was a shock to see the name of the firm, newly painted too, on the sign outside the factory and on the brass of the office entrance, newly polished. He pressed the bell at the office window inside and it was a long time before he heard footsteps cross the empty room and saw a shadow cloud the frosted glass of the window.

'It's Harold, Father,' the young man said. The door was opened.

'Hullo, old chap. This is very nice of you, Harold,' said the old man shyly, stepping back from the door to let his son in, and lowering his pleased blue eyes for a second's modesty.

'Naturally I had to come,' said the son, shyly also. And then the father filled out with assurance again and, taking his son's arm, walked him across the floor of the empty workroom.

'Hardly recognise it, do you? When were you here last?' said the father.

This had been the machine-room, now the machines had gone. Through another door was what had been the showroom where the son remembered seeing his father, then a dark-haired man, talking in a voice he had never heard before, a quick, bland voice, to his customers. Now there were only dust-lines left by the shelves on the white brick walls, and the marks of the showroom cupboards on the floor. The place looked large and light. There was no throb of machines, no hum of voices, no sound at all, now, but the echo of their steps on the empty floors. Already, though only a month bankrupt, the firm was becoming a ghost.

The two men walked towards the glass door of the office. They were both short. The father was well dressed in an excellent navy-blue suit. He was a vigorous, broad man with a pleased impish smile. The sun-burn shone through the clipped white hair of his head and he had the simple, trim, open-air look of a snowman. The son beside him was round-shouldered and shabby, a keen but anxious fellow in need of a haircut and going bald.

'Come in, professor,' said the father. This was an old family joke. He despised his son, who was in fact, not a professor but a poorly paid lecturer at a provincial university.

'Come in,' said the father, repeating himself, not with the impatience he used to have, but with the habit of age. 'Come inside, into my office. If you can call it an office now.' He apologised. 'This used to be my room, do you remember, it used to be my office. Take a chair. We've still got a chair. The desk's gone, yes, that's gone, it was sold, fetched a good price—what was I saying?' He turned a bewildered look to his son. 'The chair. I was saying they have to leave you a table and a chair. I was just going to have a cup of tea, old boy, but— pardon me,' he apologised again, 'I've only one cup. Things have been sold for the liquidators and they've cleaned out nearly everything. I found this cup and teapot upstairs in the foreman's room. Of course he's gone, all the hands have gone, and when I looked around just now to lock up before taking the keys to the agent when I hand over today, I saw this cup. Well, there it is, I've made it. Have a cup?'

'No, thanks,' said the son, listening patiently to his father. 'I have had my tea.'

'You've had your tea? Go on. Why not have another?'

'No really, thanks,' said the son. 'You drink it.'

'Well,' said the father, pouring out the tea and lifting the cup to his soft rosy face and blinking his eyes as he drank, 'I feel badly about this. This is terrible. I feel really awful drinking this tea and you standing there watching me, but you say you've had yours—well, how are things with you? How are you? And how is Alice? Is she better? And the children? You know I've been thinking about you— you look worried. Haven't lost sixpence and found a shilling, have you, because I wouldn't mind doing that?'

'I'm all right,' the son said, smiling to hide his irritation. 'I'm not worried about anything. I'm just worried about you. This—' he nodded with embarrassment to the dismantled showroom, the office from which even the calendars and wastepaper basket had gone—'this—' what was the most tactful and sympathetic word to use?— 'This is bad luck,' he said.

'Bad luck?' said the old man sternly.

'I mean,' stammered his son, 'I heard about the creditors' meeting. I knew it was your last day—I thought I'd come along, I... to see how you were.'

'Very sweet of you, old boy,' said the old man with zest. 'Very sweet. We've cleared everything up. They got most of the machines out today. I'm just locking up and handing over. Locking up is quite a business. There are so many keys. It's tiring, really. How many keys do you think there are to a place like this? You wouldn't believe it if I told you.'

'It must have been worrying,' the son said.

'Worrying? You keep on using that word. I'm not worrying. Things are fine,' said the old man, smiling aggressively. 'I feel they are fine. I know they are fine.'

'Well, you always were an optimist,' smiled his son.

'Listen to me a moment. I want you to get this idea,' said his father, his warm voice going dead and rancorous and his nostrils fidgeting. His eyes went hard, too. A different man was speaking, and even a different face; the son noticed for the first time that like all big-faced men his father had two faces. There was the outer face like a soft, warm and careless daub of innocent sealing wax and inside it, as if thumbed there by a seal, was a much smaller one, babyish, shrewd, scared and hard. Now this little inner face had gone greenish and pale and dozens of little veins were broken on the nose and cheeks. The small, drained, purplish lips of this little face were speaking.

The son leaned back instinctively to get just another inch away from this little face.

'Listen to this,' the father said, and leaned forward on the table as his son leaned back, holding his right fist up as if he had a hammer in his hand and was auctioning his life. 'I am sixty-five. I don't know how long I shall live, but let me make this clear: if I were not an optimist I wouldn't be here. I wouldn't stay another minute.' He paused, fixing his son's half-averted eyes to let the full meaning of his words bite home. 'I've worked hard,' the father went on. 'For thirty years I built up this business from nothing. You wouldn't know it, you were a child, but many's the time, coming down from the north, I've slept in this office to be on the job early next morning.' He looked decided and experienced like a man of forty, but now he softened to sixty again. The ring in the hard voice began to soften into a faint whine and his thick nose sniffed. 'I don't say I've always done right,' he said. 'You can't live your life from A to Z like that. And now I haven't a penny in the world. Not a cent. It's not easy at my time of life to begin again. What do you think I've got to live for? There's nothing holding me back. My boy, if I wasn't an optimist I'd go right out. I'd finish it.' Suddenly the father smiled and the little face was drowned in a warm flood of triumphant smiles from the bigger face. He rested his hands on his waistcoat and that seemed to be smiling too, his easy coat smiling, his legs smiling, and even winks of light on his shining shoes. Then he frowned,

'Your hair's going thin,' he said. 'You oughtn't to be losing your hair at your age. I don't want you to think I'm criticising you, you're old enough to live your own life, but your hair, you know—you ought to do something about it. If you used oil everyday and rubbed it in with both hands, the thumbs and forefingers is what you want to use, it would be better. I'm often thinking about you and I don't want you to think I'm lecturing you, because I'm not, so don't get the idea this is a lecture, but I was thinking, what you want, what we all want, I say this for myself as well as you, what we all want is ideas—big ideas. We go worrying along, but you just want bigger and better ideas. You ought to think big. Take your case. You're a lecturer. I wouldn't be satisfied with lecturing to a small batch of people in a university town. I'd lecture the world. You know, you're always doing yourself injustice. We all do. Think big.'

'Well,' said his son, still smiling, but sharply. He was very angry. 'One's enough in the family. You've thought big till you bust.'

He didn't mean to say this because he hadn't really the courage, but his pride was touched.

'I mean,' said the son, hurriedly covering it up in a panic, 'I'm not like you—I'.—

'What did you say?' said the old man. 'Don't say that.' It was smaller of the two faces speaking in a panic. 'Don't say that. Don't use that expression. That's not a right idea. Don't you get a wrong idea about me? We paid sixpence in the pound,' said the old man proudly.

The son began again, but his father stopped him.

'Do you know,' said the bigger of his two faces, getting bigger as it spoke, 'some of the oldest houses in the city are in Queer Street, some of the biggest firms in the country? I came up this morning with Mr Higgins, you remember Higgins? They are in liquidation. They are. Oh yes. And Moore, he's lost everything. He's got his chauffeur but it's his wife's money. Did you see Beltman in the trade papers? Quarter of a million deficit. And how long are Prestons going to last?'

The big face smiled and overflowed on the smaller one. The whole train, the old man said, was practically packed with bankrupts every morning. Thousands had gone. Thousands? Tens of thousands. Some of the biggest men in the city were broke.

A small man himself, he was proud to be bankrupt with the big ones; it made him feel rich.

'You've got to realise, old boy,' he said gravely, 'the world's changing. You've got to move with the times.'

The son was silent. The November sun put a few strains of light through the frosted window, and the shadow of its bars and panes was weakly placed on the wall behind his father's head. Some of the light caught the tanned scalp that showed between the white hairs. So short the hair was that his father's ears protruded and framed against that reflection of the window bars, the father suddenly took (to his son's fancy) the likeness of a convict in his cell, and the son, startled, found himself asking, 'Were they telling the truth when they said the old man was a crook and that his balance sheets were crooked? What about that man they had to shut up at the meeting, the little man from Birmingham, in a mackintosh...'

'There's a fly in this room,' said the old man suddenly, looking up in the air and getting to his feet. 'I'm sorry to interrupt what you were saying, but I can hear a fly. I must get it out.'

'A fly?' said his son, listening.

'Yes, can't you hear it? It's peculiar how you can hear everything now the machines have stopped. It took me quite a time to get used to the silence. Can you see it, old chap? I can't stand flies; you never know where they've been. Excuse me one moment.'

The old man pulled a duster out of a drawer.

'Forgive this interruption. I can't sit in a room with a fly in it,' he said apologetically. They both stood up and listened. Certainly in the office was the small dying fizz of a fly, deceived beyond its strength by the autumn sun.

'Open the door, will you, old boy', said the old man with embarrass-ment. 'I hate them.'

The son opened the door and the fly flew into the light. The old man struck at it but it sailed away higher.

'There it is,' he said, getting up on a chair. He struck again and the son struck too as the fly came down. The old man got on top of his table. An expression of disgust and fear was curled on his smaller face; and an expression of apology and weakness.

'Excuse me,' he said again, looking up at the ceiling.

'If you leave the door open or open the window it will go,' said the son.

'It may seem a fad to you,' said the old man shyly. 'I don't like flies. Ah, here it comes.'

They missed it. They stood helplessly gaping up at the ceiling where the fly was buzzing in small circles round the chord of the electric light.

'I don't like them,' the old man said.

The table creaked under his weight. The fly went on to the ceiling and stayed there. Unavailingly the old man snapped the duster at it.

'Be careful,' said the son. 'Don't lose your balance.'

The old man looked down. Suddenly he looked tired and old, his body began to sag and a look of weakness came on his face.

'Give me a hand, old boy,' the old man said in a shaky voice. He put a heavy hand on his son's shoulder and the son felt the great helpless weight of his father's body.

'Lean on me.'

Very heavily and slowly the old man got cautiously down from the table to the chair. 'Just a moment, old boy,' said the old man. Then, after getting his breath, he got down from the chair to the floor.

'You all right?' his son asked.

'Yes, yes,' said the old man, out of breath. 'It was only that fly. Do you know you're actually more bald at the back than I thought. There's a patch there as big as my hand. I saw it just then. It gave me quite a shock. You really must do something about it. How are your teeth? Do you have any trouble with your teeth? That may have something to do with it. Hasn't Alice told you how bald you are?'

'You've been doing too much. You're worried,' said the son, soft with repentance and sympathy. 'Sit down. You've had a bad time.'

'No, nothing,' said the old man shyly, breathing rather hard. 'A bit. Everyone's been very nice. They came in and shook hands. The staff came in. They all came in just to shake hands. They said: "We wish you good luck."'

The old man turned his head away. He actually wiped a tear from his eye. A glow of sympathy transported the younger man. He felt as though a sun had risen.

'You know—' the father said uneasily, flitting a glance at the fly on the ceiling as if he wanted the fly as well as his son to listen to what he was going to say—'you know,' he said. 'The world is all wrong. I've made my mistakes. I was thinking about it before you came. You know where I went wrong? You know where I made my mistake?'

The son's heart started to a panic of embarrassment. 'For heaven's sake,' he wanted to shout, 'don't! Don't start telling the truth. Don't oblige me to say we know all about it, that we have known for years the mess you've been in, that we've seen through the plausible stories you have spread, that we have known the people you've swindled.'

'Money's been my trouble,' said the old man. 'I thought I needed money. That's one thing it's has taught me. I've done with money. Absolutely done and finished with it. I never want to see another penny as long as I live. I don't want to see or hear of it. If you come in now and offered me a thousand pounds I should laugh at you. We deceive ourselves. We don't want the stuff. All I want now is just to go to a nice little cottage by the sea,' the old man said. 'I feel I need air, sun, life.'

The son was appalled.

'You want money even for that,' the son said irritably. 'You want quite a lot of money to do that.'

'Don't say I want money,' the old man said vehemently. 'Don't say it. When I walk out of this place tonight I'm going to walk into freedom. I am not going to think about money. You never know where it will come from. You may see something. You may meet a man. You never know. Did the children of Israel worry about money? No, they just went out and collected the manna. That's what I want to do.'

The son was about to speak. The father stopped him.

'Money,' the father said, 'isn't necessary at all.'

Now like the harvest moon on full glow the father's face shone up at his son.

'What I came round about was this,' said the son awkwardly and dryly. 'I'm not rich. None of us is. In fact, with things as they are we're all pretty shaky and we can't do anything. I wish I could but I can't. But'—after the assured beginning he began to stammer and to crinkle his eyes timidly—'but the idea of your being—you know, well, short of some immediate necessity, I mean—well, if it is ever a question of—well, to be frank, cash, I'd raise it somehow.'

He coloured. He hated to admit his own poverty, he hated to offer charity to his father. He hated to sit there knowing the things he knew about him. He was ashamed to think how he, how they all dreaded having the gregarious, optimistic, extravagant, uncont-rollable, disingenuous old man on their hands. The son hated to feel he was being in some peculiar way which he could not understand mean, cowardly, and dishonest.

The father's sailing eyes came down and looked at his son's nervous, frowning face and slowly the dreaming look went from the father's face. Slowly the harvest moon came down from its rosy voyage. The little face suddenly became dominant within the outer folds of skin like a fox looking out of a hole of clay. He leaned forward brusquely on the table and somehow a silver-topped pencil was in his hand preparing to note something briskly on a writing-pad.

'Raise it?' said the old man sharply. 'Why didn't you tell me before you could raise money? How can you raise it? Where? By when?'

—V.S. Pritchett

Appendix–3

The Boarding House

Mrs Mooney was a butcher's daughter. She was a woman who was quite able to keep things to herself: a determined woman. She had married her father's foreman and opened a butcher's shop near Spring Gardens. But as soon as his father-in-law was dead Mr Mooney began to go to the devil. He drank, plundered the till, ran headlong into debt. It was no use making him take the pledge: he was sure to break out again a few days after. By fighting his wife in the presence of customers and by buying bad meat he ruined his business. One night he went for his wife with the cleaver and she had to sleep in a neighbour's house.

After that they lived apart. She went to the priest and got a separation from him with care of the children. She would give him neither money nor food nor house-room; and so he was obliged to enlist himself as a sheriff's man. He was a shabby stooped little drunkard with a white face and a white moustache and white eyebrows, pencilled above his little eyes, which were pink-veined and raw; and all day long he sat in the bailiff's room, waiting to be put on a job. Mrs Mooney, who had taken what remained of her money out of the butcher business and set up a boarding house in Hardwicke Street, was a big imposing woman. Her house had a floating population made up of tourists from Liverpool and the Isle of Man and, occasionally, artistes from the music halls. Its resident population was made up of clerks from the city. She governed the house cunningly and firmly, knew when to give credit, when to be stern and when to let things pass. All the resident young men spoke of her as *The Madam*.

Mrs Mooney's young men paid fifteen shillings a week for board and lodgings (beer or stout at dinner excluded). They shared in common tastes and occupations and for this reason they were very chummy with one another. They discussed with one another the chances of favourites and outsiders. Jack Mooney, the Madam's son, who was clerk to a commission agent in Fleet Street, had the reputation of being a hard case. He was fond of using soldiers' obscenities: usually he came home in the small hours. When he met his friends he had always a good one to tell them and he was always sure to be on to a good thing—that is to say, a likely horse or a likely artiste. He was also handy with the mits and sang comic songs. On Sunday nights there would often be a reunion in Mrs Mooney's front drawing-room. The music-hall artistes would oblige; and Sheridan played waltzes and polkas and vamped accompaniments. Polly Mooney, the Madam's daughter, would also sing. She sang:

'I'm a ... naughty girl.

You needn't sham: You know I am.'

Polly was a slim girl of nineteen; she had light, soft hair and a small full mouth. Her eyes, which were grey with a shade of green through them, had a habit of glancing upwards when she spoke with anyone, which made her look like a little perverse madonna. Mrs Mooney had first sent her daughter to be a typist in a corn-factor's office but, as a disreputable sheriff's man used to come every other day to the office, asking to be allowed to say a word to his daughter, she had taken her daughter home again and set her to do housework. As Polly was very lively, the intention was to give her the run of the young men. Besides, young men like to feel that there is a young woman not very far away. Polly, of course, flirted with the young men but Mrs Mooney, who was a shrewd judge, knew that the young men were only passing the time away: none of them meant business. Things went on so for a long time and Mrs Mooney began to think of sending Polly back to typewriting when she noticed that something was going on between Polly and one of the young men. She watched the pair and kept her own counsel.

Polly knew that she was being watched, but still her mother's persistent silence could not be misunderstood. There had been no open complicity between mother and daughter, no open understanding but, though people in the house began to talk of the affair, still Mrs Mooney did not intervene. Polly began to grow a little strange in her manner and the young man was evidently perturbed. At last, when she judged it to be the right moment, Mrs Mooney intervened. She dealt with moral problems as a cleaver deals with meat: and in this case she had made up her mind.

It was a bright Sunday morning of early summer, promising heat, but with a fresh breeze blowing. All the windows of the boarding house were open and the lace curtains ballooned gently towards the street beneath the raised sashes. The belfry of George's Church sent out constant peals and worshippers, singly or in groups, traversed the little circus before the church, revealing their purpose by their self-contained demeanour no less than by the little volumes in their gloved hands. Breakfast was over in the boarding house and the table of the breakfast-room was covered with plates on which lay yellow streaks of eggs with morsels of bacon-fat and bacon-rind. Mrs Mooney sat in the straw arm-chair and watched the servant Mary remove the breakfast things. She made Mary collect the crusts and pieces of broken bread to help to make Tuesday's bread-pudding. When the table was cleared, the broken bread collected, the sugar and butter safe under lock and key, she began to reconstruct the interview which she had had the night before with Polly. Things were as she had suspected: she had been frank in her questions and Polly had been frank in her answers. Both had been somewhat awkward, of course. She had been made awkward by her not wishing to receive the news in too cavalier a fashion or to seem to have connived and Polly had been made awkward not merely because allusions of that kind always made her awkward but also because she did not wish it to be thought that in her wise innocence she had divined the intention behind her mother's tolerance.

Mrs Mooney glanced instinctively at the little gilt clock on the mantelpiece as soon as she had become aware through her revery that the bells of George's Church had stopped ringing. It was seventeen minutes past eleven: she would have lots of time to have the matter out with Mr Doran and then catch short twelve at Marlborough Street. She was sure she would win. To begin with she had all the weight of social opinion on her side: she was an outraged mother. She had allowed him to live beneath her roof, assuming that he was a man of honour and he had simply abused her hospitality. He was thirty-four or thirty-five years of age, so that youth could not be pleaded as his excuse; nor could ignorance be his excuse since he was a man who had seen something of the world. He had simply taken advantage of Polly's youth and inexperience: that was evident. The question was: What reparation would he make?

There must be reparation made in such case. It is all very well for the man: he can go his ways as if nothing had happened, having had his moment of pleasure, but the girl has to bear the brunt. Some mothers would be content to patch up such an affair for a sum of money; she had known cases of it. But she would not do so. For her only one reparation could make up for the loss of her daughter's honour: marriage.

She counted all her cards again before sending Mary up to Mr Doran's room to say that she wished to speak with him. She felt sure she would win. He was a serious young man, not rakish or loud-voiced like the others. If it had been Mr Sheridan or Mr Meade or Bantam Lyons her task would have been much harder. She did not think he would face publicity. All the lodgers in the house knew something of the affair; details had been invented by some. Besides, he had been employed for thirteen years in a great Catholic wine-merchant's office and publicity would mean for him, perhaps, the loss of his job. Whereas if he agreed all might be well. She knew he had a good screw for one thing and she suspected he had a bit of stuff put by.

Nearly the half-hour! She stood up and surveyed herself in the pier-glass. The decisive expression of her great florid face satisfied her and she thought of some mothers she knew who could not get their daughters off their hands.

Mr Doran was very anxious indeed this Sunday morning. He had made two attempts to shave but his hand had been so unsteady that he had been obliged to desist. Three days' reddish beard fringed his jaws and every two or three minutes a mist gathered on his glasses so that he had to take them off and polish them with his pocket-handkerchief. The recollection of his confession of the night before was a cause of acute pain to him; the priest had drawn out every ridiculous detail of the affair and in the end had so magnified his sin that he was almost thankful at being afforded a loophole of reparation. The harm was done. What could he do now but marry her or run away? He could not brazen it out. The affair would be sure to be talked of and his employer would be certain to hear of it. Dublin is such a small city: everyone knows everyone else's business. He felt his heart leap warmly in his throat as he heard in his excited imagination old Mr. Leonard calling out in his rasping voice: "Send Mr Doran here, please."

All his long years of service gone for nothing! All his industry and diligence thrown away! As a young man he had sown his wild oats, of course; he had boasted of his free-thinking and denied the existence of God to his companions in public-houses. But that was all passed and done with...nearly. He still bought a copy of *Reynolds's Newspaper* every week but he attended to his religious duties and for nine-tenths of the year lived a regular life. He had money enough to settle down on; it was not that. But the family would look down on her. First of all there was her disreputable father and then her mother's boarding house was beginning to get certain fame. He had a notion that he was being had. He could imagine his friends talking of the affair and laughing. She was a little vulgar; some times she said "I seen" and "If I had've known." But what would grammar matter if he really loved her? He could not make up his mind whether to like her or despise her for what she had done. Of course he had done it too. His instinct urged him to remain free, not to marry. Once you are married you are done for, it said.

While he was sitting helplessly on the side of the bed in shirt and trousers she tapped lightly at his door and entered. She told him all, that she had made a clean breast of it to her mother and that her mother would speak with him that morning. She cried and threw her arms round his neck, saying:

"O Bob! Bob! What am I to do? What am I to do at all?"

She would put an end to herself, she said.

He comforted her feebly, telling her not to cry, that it would be all right, never fear. He felt against his shirt the agitation of her bosom.

It was not altogether his fault that it had happened. He remembered well, with the curious patient memory of the celibate, the first casual caresses her dress, her breath, her fingers had given him. Then late one night as he was undressing for bed she had tapped at his door, timidly. She wanted to relight her candle at his for hers had been blown out by a gust. It was her bath night. She wore a loose open combing-jacket of printed flannel. Her white instep shone in the opening of her furry slippers and the blood glowed warmly behind her perfumed skin. From her hands and wrists too as she lit and steadied her candle a faint perfume arose.

On nights when he came in very late it was she who warmed up his dinner. He scarcely knew what he was eating feeling her beside him alone, at night, in the sleeping house. And her thoughtfulness! If the night was anyway cold or wet or windy there was sure to be a little tumbler of punch ready for him. Perhaps they could be happy together...

They used to go upstairs together on tiptoe, each with a candle, and on the third landing exchange reluctant goodnights. They used to kiss. He remembered well her eyes, the touch of her hand and his delirium...

But delirium passes. He echoed her phrase, applying it to himself: "*What am I to do?*" The instinct of the celibate warned him to hold back. But the sin was there; even his sense of honour told him that reparation must be made for such a sin.

While he was sitting with her on the side of the bed, Mary came to the door and said that the missus wanted to see him in the parlour. He stood up to put on his coat and waistcoat, more helpless than ever. When he was dressed he went over to her to comfort her. It would be all right, never fear. He left her crying on the bed and moaning softly: "*O my God!*"

Going down the stairs his glasses became so dimmed with moisture that he had to take them off and polish them. He longed to ascend through the roof and fly away to another country where he would never hear again of his trouble, and yet a force pushed him downstairs step by step. The implacable faces of his employer and of the Madam stared upon his discomfiture. On the last flight of stairs he passed Jack Mooney who was coming up from the pantry nursing two bottles of *Bass*. They saluted coldly; and the lover's eyes rested for a second or two on a thick bulldog face and a pair of thick short arms. When he reached the foot of the staircase he glanced up and saw Jack regarding him from the door of the return-room.

Suddenly he remembered the night when one of the music-hall artistes, a little blond Londoner, had made a rather free allusion to Polly. The reunion had been almost broken up on account of Jack's violence. Everyone tried to quiet him. The music-hall artiste, a little paler than usual, kept smiling and saying that there was no harm meant: but Jack kept shouting at him that if any fellow tried that sort of a game on with his sister he'd bloody well put his teeth down his throat, so he would.

Polly sat for a little time on the side of the bed, crying. Then she dried her eyes and went over to the looking-glass. She dipped the end of the towel in the water-jug and refreshed her eyes with the cool water. She looked at herself in profile and readjusted a hairpin above her ear. Then she went back to the bed again and sat at the foot. She regarded the pillows for a long time and the sight of them awakened in her mind secret, amiable memories. She rested the nape of her neck against the cool iron bed-rail and fell into a reverie. There was no longer any perturbation visible on her face.

She waited on patiently, almost cheerfully, without alarm. her memories gradually giving place to hopes and visions of the future. Her hopes and visions were so intricate that she no longer saw the white pillows on which her gaze was fixed or remembered that she was waiting for anything.

At last she heard her mother calling. She started to her feet and ran to the banisters.

"Polly! Polly!"

"Yes, mamma?"

"Come down, dear. Mr Doran wants to speak to you."

Then she remembered what she had been waiting.

—James Joyce

Bibliography

Austin, J.L. *How to Do Things with Words*, Oxford, Clarendon Press, 1962.

Barthes, R. 'Introduction to the Structural Analysis of Narratives', *Image-Music-Text*, London, Fontana, 1977.

Booth, M. *British Poetry 1964 – 1984*, London, Routledge and Kegan Paul,1985.

Brown, G. and Yule, G. *Discourse Analysis*, Cambridge, Cambridge University Press, 1983.

Brown, P. and Levinson, S. *Politeness*, Cambridge, Cambridge University Press, 1987.

Brumfit, C. and Carter, R. (eds). *Literature and Language Teaching*, Oxford, Oxford University Press, 1986.

Carter, R. (ed.). *Language and Literature: An Introductory Reader in Stylistics*, London, Allen and Unwin, 1982.

Carter, R. 'Studying Language: An Integrated Approach to Lexis in Literature', *English in Education*, Vol. 15, No.3, 1981, pp. 40 – 48.

Carter, R. and Simpson, P. *Language Discourse and Literature,* London, Unwin Hyman, 1989.

Carter, R. Walker, R. and Brumfit, C. *Literature and the Learner: Methodological Approaches*, Hong Kong, Modern English Publications and the British Council, 1989.

Crystal, D. *The Cambridge Encyclopedia of the English Language*, Cambridge, Cambridge University Press, 1995.

Crystal, D. and Davy, D. *Investigating English Style*, London, Longman, 1979.

Chapman, R. *Linguistics and Literature: An Introduction to Literary Stylistics*, London, Edward Arnold, 1973.

Chatman, S. (ed.). *Literary Style: A Symposium*, London, Oxford University Press, 1971.

Cluysenaar, A. *Introduction to Literary Stylistics:A Discussion of Dominant Structure in Verse and Prose*, London, Batsford, 1976.

Dolley, C. (ed.). *The Penguin Book of English Short Stories*, Harmondsworth, Penguin, 1967.

Finch, G. *How to Study Linguistics*, London, Macmillan Press Ltd, 1998.

Fowler, R. (ed.). *Essays on Style and Language*, London, Routledge and Kegan Paul, 1966.

Fowler, R. (ed.). *The Language of Literature*, London, Routledge & Kegan Paul, 1971.

Fowler. R. (ed.). *Style and Structure in Literature: Essays in the New Stylistics*, Oxford, Basil Blackwell, 1975.

Grice, P. 'Logic and Conversation' in Cole, P and Morgan, J (eds.) *Syntax and Semautics*, Vol. 3 New York: Academic Press, 1975.

Gower, R. 'Can Stylistic Analysis Help the EFL Learner to Read Literature?' *ELT JOURNAL, Oxford,* Vol.40, No.2, 1986.

Halliday, M.A.K. *Explorations in the Functions of Language*, London, Edward Arnold, 1973.

Halliday, M.A.K. *An Introduction to Functional Grammar*, London, Edward Arnold, 1985.

Halliday, M.A.K. and Hasan, R. *Cohesion in English*, New York, Longman, 1976.

Halliday, M.A.K. 'Linguistic Function and Literary Style: An Enquiry into William Golding's *The Inheritors*', in Chatman, S. (ed.). *Literary Style: A Symposium*, Oxford, Oxford University Press, 1971, pp. 330–65.

Halliday, M.A.K. 'Notes on transitivity and theme in English: Part I', *Journal of Linguistics*, 1967, Vol.3, pp. 37 – 81.

Hutchinson, T. 'Speech Presentations in fiction with reference to *The Tiger Moth* by H.E. Bates', in Short, M. (ed.). *Reading, Analysing and Teaching Literature*, London, Longman, 1989, pp. 120 – 145.

Jakobson, R. 'Closing Statement: Linguistics and Poetics' in Sebeok, T.A. (ed.). *Style in Language*, Cambridge, Mass. M.I.T. Press, 1960,pp. 350–77.

Leech, G.N. *A Linguistic Guide to English Poetry*, London, Longman, 1969.

Leech, G.N. and Short, M. (eds) *Style in Fiction*, London, Longman, 1981.

Labov, W. *Language in the Inner City*, Philadelphia, University of Pennsylvania Press, 1972.

McCarthy, M. and Carter, R. *Language as Discourse*, London, Longman, 1994.

Poole, S.C. *An Introduction to Linguistics*, New York, Palgrave, 1999.

Saussure, de F. *Course in General Linguistics*, 1916. Translated by Wade, B. New York, Philosophical Library, 1959.

Sebeok, T.A. (ed.). *Style in Language*, Cambridge, Mass. MIT Press, 1960.

Short, M. 'Discourse Analysis and the Analysis of Drama' in Carter, R. and Simpson, P. (eds). *Language, Discourse and Literature*, London, Unwin Hyman Ltd, 1989, pp. 139 – 168.

Short, M. (ed.). *Reading, Analysing and Teaching Literature*, Harlow, Longman, 1989.

Short, M. *Exploring the Language of Poems, Plays and Prose*, Edinburgh Gate, Harlow, Addison Wesley, Longman, 1996.

Searle, J.R. *Speech Acts: An Essay in the Philosophy of Language*, Cambridge, Cambridge University Press, 1969.

Simpson, P. *Stylistics: A Resource Book for Students*, London, Routledge, 2004.

Sinclair, J. and Coulthard, M. *Towards an Analysis of Discourse*, London, Oxford University Press, 1975.

Sundow, D. (ed.). *Studies in Social Interaction*, New York, The Free Press, 1972.

Thornborrow, J. and Shan, W. *Patterns in Language*, London, Routledge, 1998.

Toolan, M. *Narrative: A Critical Linguistic Introduction*, London, Routledge, 1988.

Toolan, M. *Language in Literature*, London, Edward Arnold, 1998.

Traugott, E.C. and Pratt, M.L. *Linguistics for Students of Literature*, New York, Harcourt Brace Jovanovich, 1980.

Turner, G.W. *Stylistics*, Harmondsworth, Penguin, 1973.

Verdonk, P. *Stylistics*, Oxford, Oxford University Press, 2002.

Walker, R. *Language for Literature*, Glasgow, Collins, 1983.

Wright, L. and Hope, J. *Stylistics: A Practical Coursebook*, London, Routledge, 1996.

Weber, J.J. (ed.). *The Stylistics Reader: From Roman Jakobson to the Present*, London, Arnold, 1996.

Widdowson, H.G. *Stylistics and the Teaching of Literature*, London, Longman, 1975.

Widdowson, H.G. *Practical Stylistics*, London, Oxford University Press, 1992.

Index